M000276948

SONDHEIM
& Me

REVEALING A MUSICAL GENIUS

bancroft
press

PAUL SALSINI
Founder of *The Sondheim Review*

Sondheim & Me: Revealing a Musical Genius

By *Sondheim Review* Founder Paul Salsini

978-1-61088-592-8 (hardcover)

978-1-61088-593-5 (paperback)

978-1-61088-594-2 (ebook)

978-1-61088-595-9 (ebook PDF)

978-1-61088-596-6 (audio)

$26.95

September 6, 2022

Cover photo © *The New York Times*

Cover & Interior Design: TracyCopesCreative.com

Author Photo: Barbara Miner

Published by Bancroft Press

"Books that Enlighten"

(818) 275-3061

4527 Glenwood Avenue

La Crescenta, CA 91214

www.bancroftpress.com

Printed in the United States of America

Other Books by Paul Salsini

NONFICTION:

Second Start

FICTION:

A Tuscan Treasury: Stories from Italy's Most Captivating Region

The Ghosts of the Garfagnana: Seven Strange Stories of Haunted Tuscany

The Fearless Flag Thrower of Lucca: Nine Stories of 1990s Tuscany

A Piazza for Sant'Antonio: Five Novellas of 1980s Tuscany

The Temptation of Father Lorenzo: Ten Stories of 1970s Tuscany

Dino's Story: A Novel of 1960s Tuscany

Sparrow's Revenge: A Novel of Postwar Tuscany

The Cielo: A Novel of Wartime Tuscany

FOR YOUNGER READERS

Stefano and the Tuscan Piazza

Stefano and the Christmas Miracles

For Barbara,
Jim, Laura, and Jack

TABLE OF *Contents*

FOREWORD

Those of us who had the great privilege of working with
Stephen Sondheim know what a huge hole his passing
created in our everyday artistic life.

There will never be enough written about this great artist,
humorist, romantic, teacher, and friend whom we called "the Boss."

He's our time's Gershwin and Shakespeare rolled into one.

He was my musical soul.

Through his work, he continues to influence
everyone he comes in contact with.

This book is another tool to try to understand his genius.

And a nice little read at that!

PAUL GEMIGNANI
May 2022

*Paul Gemignani is an American musical director whose Broadway and
West End theater career has spanned more than forty years and included more
than a dozen collaborations with Stephen Sondheim.*

PREFACE

IN 1994, I sent a letter to Stephen Sondheim telling him that I was a journalist and was about to publish a quarterly magazine devoted to his work. The magazine would include a lot of reporting, with news, articles about current and upcoming productions, reviews, interviews, and essays. As far as I knew, there had never been a publication like this devoted to a living artist.

Despite all the awards and honors and tributes Sondheim had received, I think he must have been surprised and confused by this audacious announcement. A magazine focusing on his work, and published in Milwaukee?

He apparently put his doubts aside, however, when he saw the first issue of *The Sondheim Review*—a photo of his new show *Passion* on the cover and extensive coverage inside. He said he would be willing to cooperate and gave me his contact numbers. Soon, I was calling him and he was calling me. We exchanged letters, notes, and faxes, and over the years developed an unlikely long-distance relationship.

He knew, I think, that, besides those who admired his work, the magazine would be read by scholars and historians. To make certain that every word in the magazine was accurate, he would send me notes—a wrong spelling here, confusion about a scene there. We dutifully printed his "emendations."

Except for one memorable blowup (described later in these pages), our relationship was friendly, if distant, for the ten years I was editor.

He never said so, but from his notes and our conversations, I believe he was actually pleased that *The Sondheim Review* existed and was reporting on his work.

Looking back at it now, I realize how extraordinary this personal experience was for me. I not only learned much about his work, but I also got to know something about Stephen Sondheim the genius.

In the following pages, I describe the years in which I connected with Sondheim, both before and during my time at *The Sondheim Review*. And there's more. I didn't want this to be simply Sondheim AND *The Sondheim Review*. I wanted it to be Sondheim IN *The Sondheim Review*. We reported on the many interviews, forums, and Q&A's in which he took part during those ten years as he discussed how his shows came about and how he wrote them, sometimes in very personal terms. We reported on the many productions of his work and how they were received. We devoted space to long essays that explored the depths of his work. I've excerpted or summarized many of these articles so readers can get into the mind of the musical theater's greatest composer/lyricist. Enjoy.

—Paul Salsini

INTRODUCTION

TO QUOTE Stephen Sondheim's mentor, Oscar Hammerstein II, "Let's start at the very beginning/A very good place to start."

In 1965, I took a break from my job as an editor at *The Milwaukee Journal* and my wife and I went to New York for a week. Besides the touristy things, we saw *Hello, Dolly!* with Carol Channing and *Funny Girl* with Barbra Streisand.

And, because of my love for musical theater, I wanted to see the new Richard Rodgers musical. It was now five years after Oscar Hammerstein's death, and Rodgers was striking out on his own. He had written his own lyrics for *No Strings*, but had sought someone else to write them for a new show, *Do I Hear a Waltz?*

The book, by Arthur Laurents, was adapted from his 1952 play *The Time of the Cuckoo*, which in turn was the basis for the 1955 film *Summertime* that starred Katherine Hepburn. In each case, it was the story of an American woman who falls in love with a married Italian man in Venice.

The program told us that the lyrics were written by somebody named Stephen Sondheim who, it said, had composed the lyrics for *West Side Story* and *Gypsy* and the music and lyrics for *A Funny Thing Happened on the Way to the Forum*.

Although I had seen a lot of musicals, the name didn't mean much to me. Afterward, I thought the songs in *Do I Hear a Waltz?* were pleasant enough, but I mostly remembered the pastel scenery.

Much later, I read that Sondheim had agreed to work with Rodgers only because he thought Hammerstein, his mentor and friend, would have wanted him to. It was not a happy collaboration, with Rodgers frequently browbeating his lyricist. Sondheim said many times that there was no reason for the show to exist.

Seven years later, in 1972, *The Journal* sent me to New York for a two-week journalism seminar and I had time at night to see some shows. This was before the cleanup of Times Square and it was an effort to avoid the mess in the streets, the porn shops, the unsavory characters lurking in the shadows. I tried desperately to find a show where I could feel safe.

But across Broadway there was something that looked promising. The Winter Garden Theater's marquee announced a show called *Follies* with an odd portrait of a woman with an ominous crack down her face. Still, reviewers were quoted as saying it was "breathtaking" and "incredible." I bought a ticket.

The program told me it was produced and directed by Hal Prince, that the book was by James Goldman, and the music and lyrics were by Stephen Sondheim. That name again.

When the lights went down and the music came up and tall showgirls wearing immense headpieces descended the staircase on the stage, I knew I had never seen a musical like this before. I was mesmerized.

The huge cast, the aging movie stars, the spectacular set and costumes, the lush orchestrations, the movement so continuous that it seemed like a film—it was all magical.

And then there was the score of jaunty dances, pastiche numbers, and aching ballads that revealed the characters' inner lives in sung monologues and dialogues.

Unlike so many others, this was a musical for adults.

There were so many layers to *Follies* that even now it's difficult to explain. On the surface, it was a story of two couples attending a reunion of showgirls who had been in Follies revues. But more than that, it was a story of love and loss, past and present, failure and redemption, youth and aging, missed opportunities and unforgivable mistakes. In short, it explored the follies of our lives.

I couldn't stop thinking about it and went home determined to find out more about this Stephen Sondheim. I learned that only two years earlier he wrote the score for the ground-breaking *Company,* a concept musical that had no linear plot but used vignettes to focus on a bachelor who is afraid to commit himself to others. It was nominated for a record-setting fourteen Tony awards and won six, including two for Sondheim for music and lyrics.

Somehow, I hadn't seen it.

Soon, as he wrote show after show, everyone in the 1970s seemed to be discovering Sondheim. He followed *Follies* in 1973 with *A Little Night Music,* the bittersweet story of an aging actress seeking a lost love. Counting *Company,* that made three Sondheim shows in just four years.

In 1976 came *Pacific Overtures,* focusing on, of all things, the Westernization of Japan. It was done with an all-male cast—in Kabuki style. In 1979, there was *Sweeney Todd,* the Grand Guignol story of a barber who takes revenge for being sentenced for a crime he did not commit. He kills his customers with the help of a baker who finally finds the ingredients for her meat pies.

It was a Sondheim decade. Articles and books began to appear. Scholars studied his work. He made the cover of *Newsweek*. Singers and jazz musicians recorded his songs. He was clearly the most important composer and lyricist working in the theater.

I read articles, listened to his songs, and watched videos. I collected everything I could and soon had file drawers filled. Of course, I found reasons to go to New York to see those new shows: *Night Music* (twice), *Pacific Overtures, Sweeney,* both the huge production at the Uris and the stripped-down version (dubbed *Teeny Todd*) at the Circle in the Square. I was thoroughly captivated by his works.

This all reminded me of the time a few years earlier when I became fascinated by the works of the late Wisconsin-born architect Frank Lloyd Wright. I read books, visited his buildings and homes, interviewed his widow and the architects who succeeded him, and wrote articles for the paper and even a children's book. But Frank Lloyd Wright was dead. Stephen Sondheim lived in New York. It was time to contact the source.

FIRST *Contacts*

DESPITE researching his work, there were some things that eluded me, so in April 1984, using my journalistic skills, I found Sondheim's New York address and wrote him a letter. I said that I had read much about his shows and had seen many of them, but now I was trying to find information about a musical he wrote in 1955. Never produced because of the sudden death of its producer, *Saturday Night* would have been Sondheim's first show on Broadway—when he was 25 years old. I wondered if the score had been recorded.

A week later, I received a reply, a note written on what looked like an old upright typewriter. It was on little white stationery with his name on the top.

April 26, 1984

Dear Paul Salsini –

Thanks for the lovely letter. It helps the ego no end, and at a time when ego-building is of the essence.

Enjoy the enclosed.

Yours,

(signed) Stephen Sondheim

At the time, I thought it was awfully nice of him to write, but reading it almost four decades later, I find it remarkable for several reasons.

First, the date of April 26, 1984. It was written during the tense previews for *Sunday in the Park with George,* Sondheim's newest show with a book by James Lapine, who was also directing. The show, inspired by the life of pointillist painter Georges Seurat and his masterpiece *A Sunday Afternoon on the Island of La Grande Jatte,* was to open only seven days later.

According to Lapine's *Putting It Together,* a book about the creation of the show, the opening had been delayed from April 23 to May 2 because everyone was waiting for Sondheim to write two key songs for the second act. Finally on April 25, the day before Sondheim wrote the note to me, he turned in the beautiful "Children and Art" for Marie, George's grandmother, and on April 26, the same day he wrote me, he completed "Lesson #8" for George himself.

How and why would Sondheim write to someone he'd never heard of in Milwaukee, Wisconsin, at a critical time like this?

I called Lapine to ask. He told me that because Sondheim had completed the songs, there wasn't much left for him to do in the theater, and that even after a hectic day of rehearsals and the previews, Sondheim would often sit and dictate letters to his secretary at night.

But why did he confess that he needed ego-building? Of the dozens of letters and notes I was to receive from Sondheim over the next decades, this was the most revealing.

Lapine didn't know what Sondheim meant, but said that it might have been because *Sunday* was in trouble and Sondheim was feeling the pressure. Audiences were walking out "in droves." There were hecklers.

When they heard the line "It's hot and it's monotonous" in the song "It's Hot Up Here," someone in the audience yelled, "It sure is!" The stage crew thought the show would close on opening night and called it *Sunday in the Dark and Bored.*

According to Lapine's book, Mandy Patinkin, in the role of George, confronted Sondheim: "I grabbed him by the shoulders and said, 'Write me anything. Anything! Even if it's a piece of shit. We don't care. Give us something!'"

Sondheim was aware that his two missing songs were causing panic. He told Lapine later, "I thought, everybody's depending on me. And I also had a feeling of letting you down." And also, "I'm always anxious during writing in the sense that I wonder, Can I make this work?"

There was also the fact that *Sunday* was Sondheim's first show after the abrupt failure of his *Merrily We Roll Along*, which had closed after sixteen performances three years earlier. Sondheim was so unnerved at the time that he thought about quitting musical theater, and as late as 2016 he confessed, "For the first time in my life, I felt guilty towards the cast, I felt that we had let them down."

It's probably understandable that Sondheim felt he needed "ego-building" at that time.

Despite being heavily involved in those tumultuous *Sunday* previews, he somehow found a cassette tape to send to me. At the bottom of the typewritten note, he wrote in his own hand:

P.S. The cast consists of Arte Johnson, Jack Cassidy, Alice Ghostley, Leila Martin, Jay Harnick, Robin Oliver and Richard Kallman.
SS

What he had enclosed, I discovered, was the extremely rare tape of the score of the show I'd been researching, and this was the only recording of *Saturday Night's* music and lyrics. It was from a backers' audition, a typical Broadway method to raise money when the songs are performed for potential investors. In 1953, Sondheim must have rounded up a few Broadway friends to sing the songs and he was at the piano.

I don't know if the entire score was on the tape, but I heard the rousing title song, the duet "A Moment with You," the wistful "What More Do I Need?" and the song that has since become a staple of cabaret acts, "So Many People."

Again, why did he send this to an unknown person in Milwaukee? Lapine's only response: "He was a very generous man."

MORE *Notes & Letters*

FTER GOING to New York and seeing *Sunday* later that year, I wrote to tell Sondheim how much I loved the show. I said that I, along with the rest of the audience, was overwhelmed by the glorious ending of the first act when all the characters unite to form the beautiful Seurat painting. I was, I told him, moved to tears. He replied, again on the little white stationery.

July 26, 1984
Dear Mr. Salsini –
Thanks for the terrific note. It made my day.
Gratefully,
Stephen Sondheim

I didn't know then that I was to become, like others, the recipient of many Sondheim notes over the next decades. In fact, he became known for his notes, always typewritten on his stationery and always sincere, prompt, and personal.

Except that the notes that he eventually sent to me would be in response to something in a publication about his work.

Two years later, I heard that he was working on another show with James Lapine, something about fairy tales. I sent him a tape of something or other and he responded:

November 6, 1986

Dear Mr. Salsini –

What a lovely gesture! Thank you. I think I will wait a bit to listen to the tape, at least until I finish the score to Into the Woods. *Shocks are not good for my nervous system.*

Yours gratefully,

Stephen Sondheim

I made another trip to New York, this time to see *Into the Woods*, and I sent him another congratulatory note. I said I was fascinated by the interweaving of the fairy tales, but that there was so much to think about in the show that I'd have to see it again and again. He responded:

March 18, 1988

Dear Mr. Salsini –

Thanks so much for your letter – it made me feel wonderful.

Gratefully,

Stephen Sondheim

He sent similar notes over the next years: "Thanks for the clipping. I blush."

"Thanks for the letter. It came at just the right time."

In 1991, I sent him an incisive review of *Into the Woods* and he responded:

May 3, 1991

Dear Paul Salsini –

Thanks a million for the review – you're absolutely right. Mr. Adler is the only critic who picked up on the Rapunzel story being the springboard of the entire piece.

With thanks,

Stephen Sondheim

Researching deeper into his song-writing past, I became curious about two shows, *Phinney's Rainbow* and *All that Glitters*, which Sondheim had written as a student at Williams College. In 1991, I sent him a note to ask if he could tell me about them.

The title of the first was a takeoff on *Finian's Rainbow* and referred to Williams' president, James Phinney Baxter III. The plot concerned the efforts of a fraternity at "Swindlehurst Prep" to replace physical therapy with more house parties and other less strenuous activities. Sondheim wrote the book and lyrics with a fellow student, and three songs from the show were published, "Phinney's Rainbow," "Still Got My Heart" and "How Do I Know?"

All That Glitters, the story of a young composer torn between his love for a poor girl and the prospect of marrying a rich one, was probably inspired by Rodgers and Hammerstein's *Allegro*. Hammerstein had gotten Sondheim to work as a gofer on the show during his summer vacation in 1947 and, although the show was a failure, its experimental treatment of story and characters greatly influenced Sondheim's work.

Five *Glitters* songs were published: "When I See You," "Let's Not Fall in Love," "I Love You, Etc.," "I Need Love," and "I Must Be Dreaming." I was amazed that a college student could actually write

13

musicals, that they were produced on campus, and that their songs were published.

I also asked Sondheim when the CD of his new musical *Assassins* would be released. I had seen the show in January after managing to get a single ticket for a sold-out performance at the 139-seat Playwrights Horizons theater. Like others, I admired the score but was confused by a revue-style musical about the assassinations and attempted assassinations of presidents. Opening at the same time as the start of the Gulf War, it triggered serious questions about its timing and its message. Still, there was a cast recording, and I wanted to hear the songs again.

July 25, 1991

Dear Paul Salsini

Thanks for the letter, but I fear I must disappoint you. Though Finney's (sic) Rainbow *and* All That Glitters *may have been moderately sophisticated for a college undergraduate, they're not something I would like to expose publicly. Please forgive me.*

As for the Assassins *album, it will be released in a couple of weeks, and it's terrific. I'm glad you liked the show—me, too.*

Apologetically,

Stephen Sondheim

I was probably getting obnoxious, but I persisted about the college shows. I asked if the scores were available. Sondheim responded by sending me another present.

August 7, 1991

Dear Mr. Salsini –

Unfortunately, there's no score of the college shows on file anywhere. However, a few of the songs were published and I'm enclosing duplicates of them.

Yours,

Stephen Sondheim

Amazingly, he sent me the sheet music for "How Do I Know?" and "Still Got My Heart" from *Phinney's Rainbow* and "When I See You" and "I Must Be Dreaming" from *All That Glitters*.

By this time, my interest in Sondheim's work had led me to connect with other like-minded people, even some abroad. In 1993, I was asked by the Stephen Sondheim Society (yes, there is one) in Great Britain if I would report on American productions for its newsletter. I wrote to Sondheim to let him know, and this apparently brought about a breakthrough in our fledgling relationship.

August 30, 1993

Dear Paul (we might as well be on a first-name basis) –

I'm delighted that you want to be the "American correspondent for the newsletter" but, as I warned someone over there, there may not be that much news.

As for the American productions of the shows, I rarely know about them till after they're over. I can tell you about the few "professional" ones that I know about as they arise, but I can also put you in touch with someone at Music Theater International, the organization which leases the rights to all the shows except Gypsy. He will know of every forthcoming production, from small town to university to touring, as they all have to apply for licenses from the organization (I have no "publicist").

I won't be in New York on September 10th and 11th, but in Connecticut, working furiously on a new show which starts rehearsals for a workshop two days later. Sorry about that, but if you want to talk, you can call me at xxx-xxx-xxxx (my New York number is xxx-xxx-xxxx, and please don't give either of these numbers out.)

Yours,

Steve S.

The show, I soon learned, was *Passion*. And we were now "Paul" and "Steve" and he had voluntarily given me his telephone numbers.

Meanwhile, I kept gathering information and material, and more file drawers were filling up. I didn't know what to do with all this stuff and thought briefly about writing a book, but I didn't have the time, the money, or the resources.

THE *Sondheim* REVIEW

I N JANUARY 1994, I was reading the terrific semi-annual newsletter produced by the Kurt Weill Foundation. I had long been devoted to Kurt Weill musicals, beginning with his German work, *The Threepenny Opera*, and continuing with his American musicals, including *Lady in the Dark, One Touch of Venus, Lost in the Stars*, and my favorite, the obscure *Love Life*. The newsletter reported on present and past productions and included essays about Weill's works.

It suddenly occurred to me: If a dead composer could have a newsletter, why shouldn't the world's most important composer/lyricist have one while still living and breathing? Great Britain had a Sondheim newsletter. Why shouldn't we?

At *The Milwaukee Journal*, I had become known as a speedy, well-organized editor who cut extraneous information out of copy, had good ideas for stories, and knew how to work with reporters. I was also the paper's "writing coach," a position a few papers in the country had established to help reporters with their stories. In fact, I was putting out the group's newsletter.

In one of those crazy Mickey-Rooney-Judy-Garland-let's-put-on-a-show moments, I thought that, with my background and experience, why couldn't I put out a Sondheim newsletter? At first, I thought perhaps an eight-page report issued twice a year like the Weill newsletter. At most, it could attract a couple of hundred subscribers.

The more I thought about it, the more the publication grew in my mind. There was so much to write about, and there would be so many people interested. This would not be a fanzine, though, or a scholarly journal. It would be based in journalism. It would include whatever news there was, reviews of Sondheim productions in the United States and abroad, reports on the developments of new shows and revivals, interviews with actors and directors, essays and examinations of Sondheim's work, lists of upcoming shows, and, for fun, contests, puzzles and quizzes.

And it would always be about the work, not the man.

Word got out—there are a lot of people in the Sondheim world—and instead of a little newsletter, I was now planning a quarterly magazine. I would call it *The Sondheim Review,* and now I dreamed that maybe eventually it would have thousands of subscribers.

I recruited some amazing writers and editors in New York, Chicago, Boston, Los Angeles, and elsewhere, most of whom I knew only by reputation. They were eager to take part, even without getting paid. I found a business manager in Chicago to take care of circulation, advertising—such as it was—and legal matters. I put a little money down and so did he. There was an excellent designer nearby. Also a printing plant, and I would go out there and personally supervise the printing.

I thought I'd better tell Sondheim about this, so I wrote him a letter. To my surprise, he called one Sunday afternoon—"Hi. This is Steve Sondheim"—and we talked for the first time.

He asked some questions about my proposed magazine, although I wasn't sure if he quite understood what it was all about. He did say he didn't think there would be enough to fill it, but he said well, OK, go ahead with it if you want. I took that as approval.

During that conversation, he was more interested in talking about the show he was finishing, *Passion* with James Lapine, and he was excited about it. He'd seen an Italian movie, *Passione d'Amour*, directed by Ettore Scola, and was so intrigued with its story of obsessive if unrequited love that he was using it as the basis for the musical.

Noting my surname, he wondered if I had seen the film. That, I told him, was one Italian film I'd missed. A week later, a videotape of the movie arrived in the mail—this was before DVDs. When I watched it, I could see why this story would make a powerful, dark, musical.

When we were ready to go to press with the first issue, I knew I had to get the word out about this odd magazine devoted to Stephen Sondheim's works but published in Milwaukee. I had a brilliant idea. We had *Sondheim Review* sweatshirts made and hired a guy to wear one as he distributed flyers outside the theater where *Passion* was playing in New York. It must have worked because we got subscribers.

I sent a shirt to Sondheim and he replied four days before the show's opening:

May 5, 1994

Dear Paul –

Thanks for the sweatshirt – I love those things, although wearing it in New York will seem a bit like self-advertising. But it will be terrific in the country.

Best,

Steve

PASSION

PASSION OPENED on May 9, 1994, and the first issue of *The Sondheim Review*, "Dedicated to the Musical Theater's Foremost Composer and Lyricist," was published in June. It was little more than a decade since Sondheim had first written to me, and only months after I had conceived of the idea.

The cover featured Donna Murphy and Jere Shea in *Passion*, and a letter from Sondheim appeared on page 2:

To subscribers everywhere – I'm flattered and embarrassed and delighted at your interest. I can only hope there will be enough news to justify publication.
Thanks for the support.
Happily,
Stephen Sondheim

The issue included a report on how *Passion* had changed during previews, a review of the show, and what other critics said about the score:

The New York Times: "The score contains some insinuating melodies that appear to have been forged out of cries and whispers. You can hear madness in the ecstatic lilt. The sharp drum rolls that mark the soldiers' days also could be summoning the distressed souls to order."

New York Post: "Sondheim's music—his most expressive yet—glows and glowers...From the start of his career, Sondheim has pushed the parameters of his art. Here is the breakthrough. Exultantly dramatic, this is the most thrilling piece of theater on Broadway. It will enrich you and it will touch your heart."

New York Daily News: "The score is at once one of Sondheim's most lyrical and economical...The limitations in both words and music that Sondheim seems to have imposed on himself make the expressiveness of the score all the more extraordinary. It echoes his earlier work, but with an unexpected gentleness."

In a packed issue, there were also reviews of a production of *Merrily We Roll Along* at an off-Broadway theater and of a tenth-anniversary concert of *Sunday*; reports of the touring production of *Sunday* in the U.S. and one of *Sweeney Todd* in Holland; and reviews of new CDs. I wrote a long essay on *Evening Primrose*, the 1966 television special that gave Sondheim his first national exposure. Anthony Perkins and Charmian Carr starred in this story of a poet lost among "night people" in a department store. The score included the lasting "I Remember Sky."

The coup, though, was a copy of Sondheim's score for what was called the "Train Song" from *Passion*, later known as "Loving You": "Loving you/Is not a choice/It's who I am."

I think Sondheim was impressed. At any rate, he apparently read every word because he responded to our first issue with a two-page letter.

July 18, 1994

Dear Paul –

The magazine looks classy and the articles are literate, accurate (for the most part) and not too hagiographic – congratulations. A few corrections and elucidations, however.

I should have known that was coming. The first correction referred to what I thought was an excellent and detailed report on the many changes made in *Passion* during previews.

In the piece by XXXXX about Passion *previews, he states that "When Fosca collapses in the storm scene, Giorgio originally stalked off, then returned." No, originally Giorgio never left the stage. He merely stood in angry resignation downstage left, then crossed upstage to Fosca. James (Lapine) added the stalking off later. As for the change from "ugliness" to "wretchedness", it was not intended to "make Giorgio more sympathetic to Fosca" but to take care of the fact that Donna Murphy, no matter how much prosthesis and makeup was put on her, was never able to look ugly. And the reason for the laugh on "When I die I'll leave you my braids" was that to a modern audience the notion sounds ridiculous, whereas to a 19th century audience it would have sounded natural – leaving one's hair to one's lover or family was a common legacy.*

The second correction referred to our report on the York Theater's production of the often-revised *Merrily*.

In XXXXX's report on Merrily We Roll Along, *he makes one (perfectly natural) mistake in assuming that "Not a Day Goes By" was "transferred from Franklin to his first wife, Beth." Actually, it was a reversion – the song was originally written for Beth to sing, but during previews of the 1981 production it became clear that the girl who played the part simply couldn't manage it so I had to make a quick lyric fix and gave it to Jim Walton, who could. It was always meant for Beth, whether or not Mr. XXXXX thinks it works.*

And in the elucidation department, XXXXX omits the major change in the show from all previous versions: namely, that we folded Scene 2 (which took place in a restaurant) into Scene 3 (which takes place in a television studio) in order to keep the focus more on Frank and less on Charley and Mary. Seeing this change performed for the first time in Leicester, England, in 1992 is what convinced us that the show was enough improved to make this the definitive version and to let the York Theater produce it, which I think they did in first-rate fashion.

Congratulations again,

Steve

I soon realized that this would be the norm. Sondheim would read the magazine cover to cover, perhaps circling or underlining words or phrases with one of his famous Blackwing pencils. He wouldn't spend much time in praise, but he'd write a note correcting or clarifying something that others might overlook—but not Sondheim. Every word had to be clear and correct, and there should be no confusion about anything. He obviously considered *The Sondheim Review* important because it would provide a permanent record. I took all of his comments very seriously and published them in the following issues.

SONDHEIM ON *Passion*

THE FIRST ISSUE also contained a phone interview I conducted with Sondheim just before *Passion* opened. I had seen a preview, so I knew how powerful the story was: Giorgio, a young soldier in northern Italy in the 19th century, is having an affair with a beautiful married woman, Clara. When he is transferred to an outpost, he meets Fosca, a sickly, ugly woman devastated by a brief marriage to a cad. She falls in love with Giorgio and obsessively pursues him. At first, Giorgio is repulsed, but becomes curious and then flattered. Finally, he realizes that Fosca's unconditional love is deeper than Clara's and surrenders to its power.

Sondheim began the interview by saying he was pleased with what was onstage at the Plymouth Theater. Here's our conversation.

Stephen Sondheim (SS): If you'd seen it at the beginning and seen what we did with it...I mean I didn't think it was terrible at the beginning, but it certainly changed. I think it turned out swell. I love the way it looks, I love the cast, and I love the show. I am proud of it.

The Sondheim Review (TSR): You've said that you don't want to write the same show twice, that you want a challenge. What was the challenge in writing the score for *Passion*?

SS: The idea of doing one long love song, one long rhapsody. But there's something slightly misleading here. I just saw the movie [*Passione d'Amore*] and I wanted to make a musical piece out of it without thinking for one second why. I never think why. You get attracted to a story, and you do it, for whatever series of reasons, whether they're psychological or theatrical or a combination of both. I just wanted to do it. The same thing with *Sweeney*. That's the only other time I saw something and just wanted to do it. It's always about being attracted to the story.

TSR: You've said that when you saw *Passione d'Amore* and you saw Fosca walk down those stairs, you started to cry. Is there a moment when you cry at *Passion*?

SS: Oh, there are a number of moments where I cry. Some nights, incidentally, not always. It depends on the performance.

TSR: Was there a moment of particular joy in composing the score?

SS: No. It was a hard one to write. Hard because it's one tone, has very little contrast. I knew the lyrics had to be simple, and I couldn't show off.

TSR: Did you find yourself catching yourself?

SS: No, it was just very hard to do. Worrying about the tone. The problem is to make the tone consistent throughout, and to make it rhapsodic without being boring. There's a very thin line between...it's like someone hypnotizing you and saying, "Go to sleep, go to sleep, go to sleep." Either you get hypnotized or you go to sleep.

TSR: This could have been a grand opera. But you chose not to write an opera.

SS: Yes, they're operatic-size characters, you're absolutely right. No, first of all, I don't much like opera because I like the contrast between the spoken word and the sung word. To me, the spoken word is another kind of music. And also an opera audience expects something different in the vocal production than in the character or story.

TSR: The characters are larger than life.

SS: It's like a Bette Davis, Olivia de Havilland, Errol Flynn movie. I'm just making up a Warner Bros. movie, where you have the light woman, the dark woman, and the guy in between. Many 19th century novels, particularly Italian [ones], dealt with this kind of triangle. And the fact is that "Clara" means light and "Fosca" means dark. So the literal symbolism is Tarchetti's (Iginio Tarchetti was the author of the original novel, *Fosca*.)

TSR: All the attention is on Fosca, but the story is really about Giorgio. How do you do that musically?

SS: There's nothing to answer there. I don't do anything musically. I just express the moments. Certainly at the beginning of the show, the duets between Giorgio and Clara are generally in major keys. In fact, they are in major keys, and Fosca's keys are mostly minor, and as the show progresses, the things start to switch. Not that Clara becomes minor, but Fosca starts becoming major.

TSR: The theme of love changing the object: Is that something you identify with?

SS: No, no. I'm just telling the story that Tarchetti and [Ettore] Scola told. First of all, it's mostly based on the novel. The movie follows the novel quite closely, but we really based our work on the novel, which has never been translated into English, but which we got translated into English, in a literal translation just for this purpose. The novel is quite discursive and epistolary. It is all about letters, and it is all about discussions about various aspects of love. It's one of those 19th century novels with not a lot of action and a great deal of discussion.

TSR: This has been called a chamber opera. Would you agree?

SS: Yeah, that's fair. It's not an opera. My definition of opera is something that's performed in an opera house in front of an opera audience. But operas tend to be much more through-sung than this. Even *Carmen*, which has an awful lot of dialogue, doesn't have as much dialogue as this. This show has, unlike, say, *Sweeney,* the average amount of dialogue. If you took the proportion of dialogue to song, the aural illusion comes from the persistent underscoring, which gives the impression, like *Sunday in the Park with George,* that a lot of it is sung. In fact, the percentage of sung to spoken here is no different than *Oklahoma!* or, you name it. But the underscoring is fairly constant.

TSR: Can you talk about the problems some audiences were having during the previews.

SS: The audience laughed at twenty places where we didn't want them to. That's because our Fosca was much like the character in the movie. In the film, she looks like a walking skeleton and her hysteria is frightening. Here, she's an operatic-sized character in a musical. And though *Passion* is not an opera because it has so much dialogue, it is an opera in attitude. If this were all sung, and it were done at the Metropolitan Opera House, no one would laugh. You'd accept it. We red-flagged each moment where the audience laughed, and we'd change a word or two or change the lighting. We softened Fosca by doing an enormous amount of work on the tone of the piece. There are no scenes we cut. We didn't throw out song after song.

TSR: What changes were made?

SS: One aspect of the finale has changed where Fosca realizes she's "someone to be loved." We changed one of the letters Clara writes Giorgio. Before, she dumped him; now, he takes charge in ending their affair. And we added a song on the train for Fosca, which helps the audience understand why her obsession with Giorgio "is not in my control."

TSR: Because of the way the score is written, the audience doesn't have a chance to applaud.

SS: I didn't want the show to have breaks for applause after each song. I wanted it to play like one long rhapsody. But that meant there was no place for people to release their tension. This is the first show I've written with no irony. The characters have no humor—actually,

Fosca does. People say it breaks new ground. I say, yes, as the world's first humorless musical.

>   *TSR*: You're satisfied with *Passion* now?
>   **SS**: Yeah, I like it a lot.

PASSION *Interviews*

THE SECOND ISSUE, Fall 1994, was published three months later with an assessment of the score of *Passion* by the highly respected music critic David Patrick Stearns. He wrote: "After seeing the show in the theater three times, I was confident that it was among his very best scores. Now, I'd venture to say it's THE best. Lyrics, music, and dialogue have never been more integrated. His musical characterizations have never been so keen. Above all, *Passion* is—by far—his most deeply felt score."

There were also interviews with the stars. I called Donna Murphy:

"Much has been written," I said, "about the rocky reception *Passion* got in previews, the unintended laughter, etc. Were you surprised by the rudeness of some of the audiences?"

"Oh, yeah," Murphy replied. "I have to be honest. I don't begrudge their response, but what makes me angry is when they feel they have to let everyone else know: 'I think this sucks.' It's rude to the rest of the audience, who should be allowed to have their own experience. At one show, when Fosca faints and Giorgio starts to leave her, maybe a dozen people started clapping. I was on the floor, hoping it would open up and take me down. But as Giorgio crossed back over to me, another group started to clap for me."

"What," I asked, "do you think were some of the most important changes?"

"The ones in the train scene. It's the moment in the show when the audience needs to see Giorgio shift his perspective of Fosca. And they have to do the same. The seeds were there from the very beginning, but they needed to be spelled out…Then the scene started to change, which eventually led to 'Loving You' in which Fosca explains to Giorgio, 'Loving you is not a choice, it's who I am,' but it wasn't just the insertion of a song. We know how Giorgio is cracked open by her love, but if Fosca doesn't learn something more from all of this, we have a problem."

Some critics had thought that Giorgio's transition from revulsion to attraction to Fosca was too abrupt, so I asked Jere Shea if he thought it was a gradual thing.

"Some people see the turning point in the train scene," he said. "I think that's where it's a little more obvious, but I think it happens earlier. I think he starts to experience feelings for this woman, you might call it compassion, especially in the bedroom scene where she grabs him and kisses him. I always referred to that as a vampire kiss, planting something like a virus. So that by the time the train scene comes around, you can say, 'Oh, this guy has got something, he's caught it.' It becomes more obvious that I'm becoming more like Fosca."

I interviewed Marin Mazzie over lunch at a midtown restaurant. Needless to say, I didn't eat much. She was gracious and eager to talk about her role as Clara. (Marin Mazzie died on September 13, 2018, after a three-year battle with ovarian cancer.)

She said she carried Clara around in her head all day. "I live that every day and every night. So I go out on stage there's a different scenario or a different theme, with Clara's husband or with Giorgio. And the material is so great that it allows new discovery."

How do audiences respond to Clara, a woman who won't leave her husband for Giorgio until her son is older?

"I think people are sympathetic, perhaps not to her as a person but the situation she is in. After all, this is 1863, and it's not easy doing what she's doing. I think people can look at her and relate to what she's going through and feel compassion."

Passion closed the following January after 280 performances. It won Tony awards for best musical, Sondheim's score, and Lapine's book. Donna Murphy won for best actress in a musical.

Sondheim's response to the second issue was brief.

October 19, 1994

Dear Paul –

I enjoyed Issue #2 very much, and even learned some things I didn't know. One erratum: It's Jane Greenwood, not Joan, who designed the costumes for Passion. *Joan was a well-known British actress.*

Steve

The mistaken first name was deep in the interview with Marin Mazzie. Was that all he found? I wondered why the note was so short, but realized that *Passion* was in trouble then and he was probably preoccupied. Or maybe there wasn't anything else to correct.

TALKING WITH *Students*

I N NOVEMBER 1994, Southern Methodist University in Dallas announced that it would present Sondheim with its prestigious Algur H. Meadows Award for Excellence in the Arts. A week of sessions with students was also planned, and there would be a concert in which students would perform and Bernadette Peters would sing "Not a Day Goes By" with Sondheim at the piano.

Naturally, I had to go to Dallas to cover this event. Because *TSR* had no budget for hotels, I freeloaded at the home of a friendly editor at the *Dallas Morning News.*

The following was the lead article I wrote in the Winter 1995 issue:

WE'VE READ about Oscar Hammerstein's enormous influence as a mentor for Stephen Sondheim. We've heard of Sondheim's tributes to his teachers and to the others who guided him as a young composer; Sondheim admits, in fact, that he gets teary-eyed when he thinks about the role of teacher.

After five days at Southern Methodist University in November, it is easy to imagine Sondheim himself as teacher, handing over to young people the knowledge and experiences that profoundly influenced his own life.

Slightly rumpled in pullover and slacks and comfortably slouched in a wooden chair, Sondheim was the classic inspired teacher—getting excited about ideas, telling stories about his shows and his colleagues, describing his own creative processes, giving advice on getting established, encouraging the students' ideas. Like the three young idealists in *Merrily We Roll Along*, the students discovered the infinite possibilities of opening doors.

What follows is a compilation of Sondheim's responses to student questions on various topics.

THE CREATIVE PROCESS

You've been accused of writing cold characters. How did you come to express the great emotion of a Sweeney or a Fosca?

You have to be an actor. I become the actor or actress playing the part. It's not about me, it's about how actors play the part. And it's not so much forcing myself into it, but imitating. Playwrights and composers should know the characters as thoroughly as the actors who play them.

Do you use lines from librettists?

I rob the librettists all the time. For the opening of *Sunday*, James [Lapine] wrote out a monologue for Dot, complete with the sweat rolling down her neck, and that became the lyrics. The same with "Color and Light." I asked James what George and Dot would be thinking, and he wrote lines knowing they would never be spoken.

I like to put the dialogue on the piano like a score and sing it. I want the music to reflect the dialogue. And sometimes you find a line that you can steal for a song, or use with the underscoring.

When do you start writing the songs?

I usually don't start the lyrics until I've seen several scenes. I don't mind writing a bad song because it won't get out of my living room, but I don't want to write a wrong song.

How do you balance the music and the dialogue?

That's something you struggle with during rehearsals. James always wants more music, and I always want more dialogue, so you have two kinds of neurotic protesters. When you get to rehearsal, you realize such things as "Why didn't that character sing for the last twenty minutes?"

What attracts you to an idea for a show?

It's the story, it's always the story. I think any story is worth telling. But halfway through, you realize why you're telling the story, and that's why the songs at the end sum up what you're trying to say. I started realizing that was happening when I was writing *Sweeney*. I rarely discover what the show is about until halfway through. I don't think I could have written "Children and Art" without seeing the whole show.

What's your working schedule?

I established my work habits in college, and tended for years to write late at night. Now I start about 11 in the morning and work eight-to-twelve hours a day, seven days a week. I am a firm believer in the unconscious solving problems in sleep. I try to limit any kind of extracurricular activity when I face a deadline, which is about two months before the workshop begins. I find that just talking to people is a distraction. I can write about one song a week.

What kind of research do you do for your shows?

I don't like to read an awful lot, so I don't do much research. For *Follies*, Jim Goldman and I went to a reunion of Follies girls. For *West Side Story*, Jerry [Robbins] and I went to a gang dance. Jerry noticed that all the girl members of one gang presented carnations to the guys, who put them in the cuffs of their pants. So Jerry tried that in the dance scene—and carnations were flying all over the stage and people were ducking. That was the end of the research.

For *Funny Thing [Happened on the Way to the Forum]*, I read *Daily Life in Ancient Rome*, which was very helpful. For *Pacific Overtures*, I read books about Japan. For *Sunday*, we read about Seurat—and fortunately there wasn't very much. We went to Chicago for a couple of days to view the painting, and we heard people actually say, "It's made of little dots!"

For *Sweeney Todd*, I tried to find British slang, but I had to make up the dirty dialogue for the Beggar Woman. For *Company*, since I haven't been married, I talked with Mary Rodgers, who was married twice. I know about relationships, but not marriage.

COMMENTS ABOUT SHOWS

Could you please comment about some of your shows?

Assassins: This was the first time that I didn't see a few scenes first. John [Weidman] wrote the entire draft before I saw it. I read it and couldn't wait to start writing. I wrote it chronologically, and I knew the styles I wanted to use. For "Unworthy of Your Love," I was going to use Patti Smith, but then I used the Carpenters. *Assassins* opened at a time of great patriotism in the country and the critics slammed it. It was unfairly treated. I'm still angry about that.

Do I Hear a Waltz?: There was no reason to do that show.

Sunday in the Park with George: [*In response to a question about the second act being less successful than the first*] The first act is a stunt. It wouldn't be worth writing without the second. We had other plans for the second act; it was going to be a history of the painting over 100 years, with the various descendants. I wanted to open the act outside of Central Park with the Shakespeare Festival, which would have been the equivalent of the Grand Jatte. But it developed differently. If you feel the second act is faulty, it's because the first act tells an inevitable story, and the second moves around in time and space. The last ten minutes move the most. We fine-tuned it as much as we wanted to; it's totally satisfactory.

Company: (*If he were writing* Company *today, would he include a lesbian or gay couple?*) That might be possible, but it would also be a cliché. *Company* is about contractual relationships, commitments by paper. There was a move to "modernize" it for the 25th anniversary revival, but I said no.

The Frogs: Burt Shevelove asked me to do it when he was at Yale, and I owed him a favor so I said yes. It has only six songs. It's a university piece. I think it's quite good, but I have no desire to expand it.

Anyone Can Whistle: It's a very flawed show, but I don't know how I would improve it. I could write three pages of what's wrong, but at the same time, I'm not ashamed of the show. When it closed, I thought I would be destroyed, but I was only disappointed—so many people I knew wouldn't have a chance to see it.

Into the Woods: It's a brilliantly plotted farce, like *Forum.* Every single action happens because of a single premise for it.

FROM STAGE TO SCREEN

Please comment on the film versions of your musicals.

West Side Story was radically changed. *Gypsy* was opened up a little, and *A Funny Thing Happened on the Way to the Forum* neglected the thing that makes the show work, its narrative line.

What's funny about *Forum* is not the lines, but the situations, and the situations only arise if you tell the story properly. The result, for example, is the climactic 15-minute chase scene, which is singularly unfunny despite the fact that Buster Keaton is in it. It's unfunny because you don't know what's at stake; nobody needs anything, it's just a bunch of sight gags.

Although *West Side Story* was an enormous hit, I don't think the picture's any good. It's got no style. The whole point of *West Side Story* is not juvenile delinquency. It's about the theater, about ways of telling the story. It's not about character, it's about plot, and how to tell it, how to mix dialogue and music, how to mix dance. It's a remarkable, sophisticated mix of theater techniques. But if you're going to do a movie, you've got to find equivalents. They didn't find a *West Side Story* style, they didn't find a *Gypsy* style. In *Forum,* they found a style, but it was the wrong one.

A *Little Night Music* should never have been done. It's dreadful. Hal [Prince] is a great stage director, but he's not a movie director.

Which of your other shows would work as a film musical?

Company. It's a series of episodes, and it's very much influenced by cross-cutting. But if it were done, I would want it changed. I think it would be very important to be rethought.

What do you think of movie musicals in general?

I've never seen a stage musical that was satisfactory on screen. What the stage does is stretch out time. What film does is compress time. Thus, even if someone is sitting on the stage and singing for three or four minutes, it will hold your attention. It's a convention the audience accepts. As soon as people start to sing to each other in movies, you've got a problem.

ABORTED PROJECTS

Sondheim was asked about projects that had been announced but not completed.

Muscle (planned as part of a double bill with *Passion*, it was the story of a young man obsessed with body building). "Both *Muscle* and *Passion* are about appearances and obsession, and we thought they might go together. I did about five pieces of music for *Muscle*, but it needs contemporary sounds and it's not me."

Singing Out Loud (a proposed movie with Rob Reiner for which Sondheim wrote six out of eight songs, including "Water Under the Bridge"). "This is so much on a back-burner I don't think it will ever heat up. I don't think the movie will ever be made."

The Chorus Girl Murder Case (a movie that was supposed to be directed by Michael Bennett with a script by Sondheim and Anthony Perkins, and Tommy Tune as the hero). "We wrote 80 pages of treatment, including a lot of dialogue, and there would have been twelve musical numbers, each leading to a clue. But Michael either decided not to do it or didn't get the backing. It's fun, but it's sitting on a shelf."

MISCELLANEOUS MATTERS

You were an actor in college. If you were a singer and actor, what character in your shows would you like to play?

I'd rather die than sing on stage. Well, I'd love to play Sweeney, or Seurat, or Franklin Shepard. But I'd really not like to play any of them. I'd like to watch others play them.

Among the songs you've written, which are your favorites?

I don't have a favorite, but there are some that I like a lot—"Someone in a Tree," and "Opening Doors," which is the only autobiographical song I've ever written.

I heard you like country music.

Yes, it's short, rueful, and a word I don't like, clever. There's a spirit about country music that I like.

Will we ever hear a Stephen Sondheim country song?

No.

More LETTERS

W̲E ALSO BROKE SOME NEWS in our Winter 1995 issue. We announced that Sondheim was working on a new musical that would be both big and fun. In a phone call, he said he had the idea for the show when he was 22, that he would be working with John Weidman, and that it would be based on two brothers he declined to name.

He said it would be "very musical comedy, very jazzy, very bright and funny," would incorporate more dance than usual, and have a full orchestra. He said the show would have a workshop in the fall of 1995, and if that went well, rehearsals would start in January 1996, and the show would open in the spring of 1996 at the Kennedy Center in Washington.

In his note about the issue, Sondheim's main comments were about a review of the cast album of *Merrily We Roll Along* by the Haymarket Theater in Leicester, England, although they were more about the liner notes for the CD than our review.

January 3, 1995

Dear Paul –

The new issue looks very good indeed. Congratulations again.

However, XXXXX's report on the liner notes for the British Merrily We Roll Along *is unfortunate. The notes are almost ludicrously incorrect, as is XXXXX's report that Mary (!) is the iodine-thrower. Incidentally, I agree with his assessment of the recording, but the irony is that the cast in Leicester was wonderful. The problem lies with the record producer, who is notorious for doing shows that nobody else is recording (which is good) but on the cheap (which is bad). One of the results of the latter is that he was so anxious to rush the long-delayed recording into release that he didn't let me vet the liner notes. I've asked XXXXX, the writer, to correct the numerous errors, if there ever should be a reprinting. Meanwhile, tell your readers not to pay any attention to the notes whatsoever—including the "historical" ones.*

Sondheim also commented on our postmortem on *Passion* in which we quoted several authorities on why they thought it closed after a fairly short run, among them *New York Times* theater critic Frank Rich.

To satisfy my own curiosity, I'd love to know where Frank Rich's quotes about Passion *come from.*

There was a simple answer to that. Like any good journalist, I just called Frank Rich and asked him. He said he thought the fact that *Passion* closed after only a seven-month run said more about Broadway than about *Passion*. "The audience for a sophisticated, intellectual show, which is what *Passion* is, is good only for a few months."

Sondheim ended with this:

Again, in spite of these things, congratulations. Happy New Year to all of us.

Steve

The next Sondheim note to me included an apology. I had gone to New York to see *Passion* again before it closed but missed Sondheim.

January 27, 1995

Dear Paul –

Sorry to have missed you in New York, but I was up to my neck with the filming of Passion *and another project, of which you'll be hearing shortly.*

Best,

Steve

I assumed the project was the "very musical comedy" he had told us about earlier. He was still being mysterious about it.

IN OUR SPRING 1995 issue, we reported that Sondheim and George Furth were collaborating on a murder mystery—without songs. Previously, they had worked together on *Company* and *Merrily We Roll Along*. Tentatively titled *Getting Away with Murder*, the play was to be about a therapy group without a psychiatrist.

We quoted Sondheim:

"I mentioned a plot idea to George Furth a couple of years ago, he showed enthusiasm, and I asked him to invent a set of characters for the situation. He wrote an act and the beginning of a second, and then bogged down because of plot complications. I told him I would get to it after *Passion* opened, and I did.

"I spent the months of August, September, and October rewriting what he had done and writing the second act. Then we collaborated via phone, changing and cutting where necessary.

"Since I did this primarily for fun, I had no intension of its ever leaving the living room, but I showed it to a number of professional friends, and their reaction was so enthusiastic that we had a reading [under its original title, *The Sins of the Fathers.*]"

The show was to premiere at the Old Globe Theater in San Diego, September 16-21, 1995.

We also reported that Sondheim's mysterious musical project was about Wilson and Addison Mizner, two eccentric brothers who developed Palm Beach and Boca Raton in the 1920s. Several books had been written about the Mizners, but Sondheim said he and John Weidman had done their own research in the Palm Beach Historical Society because "their lives were so flamboyant that they inevitably bred a great deal of apocrypha."

Work on the show was interrupted by a devastating fire at Sondheim's New York townhouse on February 24, 1995. He was not at home at the time. Although his original manuscripts were spared, the fire destroyed an accumulation of supplies and records in his office. We also reported that his "fluffy, friendly poodle Max was killed."

Also in the issue was an extraordinary batch of passages from Martin Gottfried's gorgeous coffee-table book *Sondheim.* Gottfried himself selected the sections and explained that they had to be cut from the book "or the retail price would have been $100."

There was also a five-page analysis of *Do I Hear a Waltz?*, that early show for which Sondheim wrote the lyrics to Richard Rodgers' music. The author concluded: "Compared to their greater works, *Waltz* is lifeless and dull. Though it has more than a few endearing moments, it is, on the whole, a low point in both Sondheim's and Rodgers' careers."

Sondheim didn't argue that point but, in his note to me, elaborated on other aspects of the article in his response to the issue.

April 28, 1995

Dear Paul –

Here are a couple of responses and comments to articles in the Spring issue.

Passion, which we just finished editing, has turned out superlatively partly because it's on film and not on tape, unlike all other shows that have undergone similar treatment.

Max was indeed a poodle, but not a "fluffy" one—he was a Standard.

The article on Do I Hear a Waltz? *slightly maligns Richard Rodgers. He treated me very well until we got to New Haven and the show was in trouble.*

As for the "unclear" history of the project, here are the facts: Arthur Laurents wanted Rodgers and Hammerstein to adapt The Time of the Cuckoo, *in the late fifties, and to this end I introduced Arthur to Oscar. Oscar was greatly taken with the idea, but felt that both the play and the movie [*Summertime*] had been too recent, and that he would like to wait about five years before embarking on the show. A couple of years later, he died, and Arthur suggested to Rodgers that he do the show with me. Rodgers had been offering me numerous projects since Oscar's death, none of which appealed to me (mostly because I wanted to be my own composer). But this one had the advantage of the collaboration with Arthur and the fulfillment of a promise I had made to Oscar before he died—he assumed that Dick was going to be sorely in need of a collaborator and hoped that I, in spite of my ambitions to be a composer, would find something mutually agreeable to us.*

The observation that "This Week Americans" (from Do I Hear a Waltz?*) merely sounds bigoted is precisely the point: Fioria was intended* *to be a bigoted character. And the observation that there's "apparently no irony" in the lyrics of "We're Gonna Be All Right" strikes me as odd: what else could it be but ironic since the audience knows the circumstances of Eddie and Jennifer's fragile and self-deceptive marriage. The lyrics may not look ironic on the surface, but that's the way they played in the theater.*

Congratulations on another good issue—I was particularly impressed and entertained by the article on casting Follies.

As always,

Steve S.

In that last line, Sondheim was referring to a contest we had sponsored in the previous issue: cast *Follies* as an all-star movie. We received dozens of entries, with some contestants making up posters, choosing directors, and going farther down the cast list than we had suggested.

If we had gone by popular votes, Shirley Jones would have been Sally, Kevin Kline would have been Ben, Glenn Close or Julie Andrews would have played Phyllis, Dick Van Dyke would have gotten the nod for Buddy and Lena Horne for Carlotta.

The winning entry, we determined, had Meryl Streep as Sally, Jeremy Irons as Ben, Glenn Close as Phyllis, Ron Silver as Buddy, and Elizabeth Taylor as Carlotta.

COMPANY *Revived*

ON OCTOBER 5, 1995, the first revival of *Company* arrived on Broadway with Boyd Gaines as Bobby and Debra Monk as Joanne. We devoted almost the entire Fall 1995 issue to it, including a review that concluded: "The bottom line is that, *Company*, you'll always be what you always were: a masterpiece of musical theater with a new production that does you proud."

Other critics, however, had reservations:

The New York Times: "Though you may be so familiar with the Sondheim music and lyrics that you can play them in the mind at will, the show itself doesn't look or behave exactly as imagined...As with a newly met pen pal, you have to make allowances. Not, heaven knows, for some of the most dazzling and bittersweet show tunes Mr. Sondheim has ever written."

Newsday: "[Scott] Ellis' production is a bright, confident, entertaining testament to one of the greatest scores ever to revolutionize the stage....Perhaps we need this show too much and know it too well ever to be completely satisfied with a revival. This one is a good *Company*, which, on Broadway is far better company that most."

TheaterWeek: "The revival is an up and down, uneven affair, sometimes satisfying, elsewhere disappointing, and perhaps more interesting for the questions it raises than the ones it answers."

We also talked to the stars of the original 1970 production.

Dean Jones, who left the role of Bobby for personal reasons early in the run, said: "Steve made an indelible impression upon my life. He's one of the most uniquely gifted men I've ever met. And such courage he has, to be so open with his feelings! I don't have that kind of courage. Steve writes these wonderfully deep, profound things down for everyone to see. And you know he's feeling them because they ring so true in our hearts."

Elaine Stritch, the unforgettable Joanne, also talked about Sondheim.

"He's scary, Steve. I think he's very close to a genius, if not genius, and it's hard to be around people like that. They're mind-boggling, their talent is so explosive, and there's a kind of a dangerous quietness about them. But, boy, I'll tell you about Steve Sondheim. When you get it right, no one is ever as happy. And that's where you get to have a real relationship with another artist. He really lets you have it. He's terrible when you're not with it, but when you get it right, he is so overjoyed by the material being interpreted the way he saw it that he makes you feel like a million bucks.

"He wrote me a note that I still have after I sang 'Ladies Who Lunch' in front of this small audience of big shots, and he told me that I had turned a song that might be sung after hours in a piano bar into a piece of theater. So what do you do with that kind of compliment? I remember I celebrated that letter by having four martinis before dinner."

There was talk of moving the show from the nonprofit, subscription-based Roundabout Theater to a larger, commercial Broadway house, but a very public fight developed between the producer, John Hart, on the one hand, and Sondheim and the director, Scott Ellis, on the other. Hart wanted to replace Boyd Gaines and suggested other changes. Sondheim and Ellis vetoed them, and Sondheim issued a rare public statement saying Hart "has no experience as a producer, only as a money man."

He added: "In the case of *Company*, every time we [the show's creators, stagers, designers, agents, etc.] agreed to his terms, he would ask for more cast replacements, more restaging and rewriting, until it became apparent that he didn't really want to move the show. My guess is that he couldn't raise the necessary money."

The show closed on December 3 after 111 performances, including 43 previews. It was nominated for a Tony award for best revival of a musical but did not win.

In view of the gender-bending *Company* on Broadway in 2021, a report from Seattle in that issue seems relevant now. The Alice B Theater, a gay and lesbian group, produced a version that had Bobby, a gay man, bedding a male flight attendant; "Harry" becoming "Harriet" and fighting with "Sarah," and "Peter" being gay but married to "Susan."

Music Theater International sent a cease-and-desist letter, and Sondheim said he found out about it too late. He told us: "If George [Furth] and I had meant to write a gay central character, we would have. But many directors and producers who can't write, rewrite."

Later, we reported on a gender switch in another *Company* production. In performances at Pittsburgh's Carnegie Mellon University, director Billy Porter switched "Marta" to a "Marty," who was trying to pry Bobby out of the closet, but Bobby wouldn't leave. So instead of Bobby's resistance to commitment being traceable to unacknowledged homosexuality, as many had imagined, it became more a resistance to commitment, period.

Asked about the change, Sondheim told *TSR* that he gave Porter permission to do this because it was only a college production. "This doesn't mean it could be done elsewhere, and in no way should it be viewed as a blueprint for future productions."

In his next note, Sondheim commented on both the Fall and the subsequent Winter issues and volunteered a story about a production of *Sweeney Todd* he'd seen.

January 12, 1996

Dear Paul –

Dept. of Corrections and Emendations:

In reference to the Fall issue, David Shire did more than "new orchestrations" on "Tick Tock"—he wrote the music. And anent the ending of Company *in Boston, Bobby was not sitting on a park bench but by a pool. And he was not approached by a "previously unseen person, a member of the vocal minority," but by Teri Ralston, playing (as did everybody else) a character different from the one she had played during the course of the show. And despite Hal [Prince's] recollection, the reason the show was cut was that it was a half hour too long.*

In the Winter issue, on p. 8 the lyric should read, "It's not talk of God and the moon" (not mood).

And readers might be interested to know that I went to Barcelona to see the Catalan production of Sweeney Todd *that gave rise to the recording mentioned on p. 29, and it was one of the most thrilling experiences I've ever had in the musical theater: full of ferocious energy, over-the-top performances (even the set made the actors look larger than life) and brilliantly detailed staging (they had three months to rehearse, as opposed to the American five weeks' worth and the British eight).*

Keep up the good work.

As always,

Steve

$\mathcal{F}orum$ REVIVED

THE SPRING 1996 issue included a review of the Sondheim-Furth murder mystery *Getting Away with Murder*, which was blasted by critics and closed after seventeen performances; a Q&A with Mandy Patinkin; the views of a psychologist on Sondheim's lyrics; and a Q&A with Nathan Lane, who was about to star in a revival of *A Funny Thing Happened on the Way to the Forum*.

Lane had played Pseudolus when he was 18 and Hysterium when he was 19, and he told Jerry Zaks, the director for whom he starred in *Guys and Dolls*, that he wanted to do *Forum* again.

"It's got the funniest book ever written for a musical," Lane told us. "It's a tremendous amount of fun. And I love the score, which is underrated. [Sondheim] said to me the other day at the first read-through, 'Oh, I was showing off. If I were writing it today, I would do it differently.' And I said, 'No, it holds up pretty well.' He was very funny about it.

"I love 'Free.' And the whole evening is really built upon it. I love 'Everybody Ought to Have a Maid.' It always brings down the house. It's a witty and wonderful vaudeville number. We're doing 'That'll Show Him,' which sometimes has been substituted by 'Echo Song.' And we're doing just a little more of 'The House of Marcus Lycus,' using some additional lyrics."

We reported that Sondheim discarded more songs for *Forum* than for any other show he had written. That said nothing about their quality; it was simply that *Forum*'s plot changed drastically over the four years—and ten rewrites—that it took Burt Shevelove and Larry Gelbart to finally become satisfied with their work.

A good deal of what was once called *A Roman Comedy* remains in the final version, but when plot turns were revised and the plot itself refined, some characters were gone. Vino, a playboy originally named Inebrium and described as "slightly intoxicated throughout," did not survive the third rewrite. A Money Lender and a Brothel Servant were also left behind. Gusto's name changed to Hero and Lovlia's to Philia.

A hint of what might have been can be found in the Wisconsin Center for Film and Theater Research, part of the Wisconsin Historical Society collection in Madison. In 1967, like other theater people at the time, Sondheim donated his early papers to the collection. Madison is ninety miles from Milwaukee, so I drove over to look at them.

There, on yellow-and-yellowing legal-pad paper, were his hand-written sketches for many songs. Words were crossed out, new ones added; more scribbled words were in the margins, on the sides, on the bottom. A study of the pages revealed Sondheim's well-known meticu-lous process of finding exactly the right word, the right rhyme.

In one plan, Sondheim would have written twenty-six songs (there are fifteen in the final version of *A Funny Thing Happened on the Way to the Forum*). The Procurer would have a "Hymn to Venus." The Lecherous Father would declare that "It's Nice to Have a Girl Around the House." The Courtesan and the Playboy would sing a "material-istic love song—the little things that count—such as rings, etc." The Hysterical Slave would find that "The House Is Haunted." The big production number would have been a "Banquet Song," with "sections for all."

In the Madison archives are fragments of twenty-one unused songs, and some are more fragmented than others. Only a few lines were written for "Seven Hills of Rome" and "Take the Acorn," and others materialize into songs that were used. "Happy Endings" was an early version of "Invocation":

Let the comedy start
With the rumble of doom.
Make it serious art
Give it glower and gloom.
One thing only we ask—
When you've given it these,
Give it a happy ending, please.

The revival was warmly greeted by many critics. *The New York Times* critic wrote:

"This brazenly retro Broadway musical, inspired by Plautus, is almost as timeless as comedy itself. Here's a glorious, old-fashioned farce with its vintage Stephen Sondheim score and its breathless book by Burt Shevelove and Larry Gelbart, that celebrates everything that man holds least dear but cannot deny himself: lust, greed, vanity, ambition, in short, all of those little failings that make man human."

To balance the coverage, *The Sondheim Review* also carried a piece entitled "Forum: classical, prophetic...and also sexist."

"The female characters in *Forum* are defined by the stereotypes of the 'dumb blonde,' the 'shrewish wife,' and the 'sex object.' Along with the sexist role modeling of the female characters, the male characters treat the females with little respect. And then, of course, there is the advice that everyone ought to have a maid ('appealing in her apron strings/beguiling in her blouse').

"Certainly," the author continued, "most of that plot structure is the responsibility of the book writers, Burt Shevelove and Larry Gelbart, but Sondheim does not work on projects that do not speak to him."

Lane, who won a Tony award for his performance, was succeeded by Whoopi Goldberg and then David Alan Grier and *Forum* ran for 715 performances.

AN UNUSUAL *Encounter*

ALONG WITH the *Forum* coverage in that same Spring 1996 issue, we carried a report/review of the London production of *Passion* starring Michael Ball as Giorgio, Maria Friedman as Fosca, and Helen Hobson as Clara.

Although British critics had generally praised Sondheim's work in the past, some were not kind to *Passion*. Our piece reported that they called *Passion* "pretty but vapid" but also "stylishly directed." The score was labeled a "bittersweet beauty" and a "piece from the heart" but also "irritatingly cool," "dispassionate," and "remorsefully academic."

The London critics praised Maria Friedman's performance but found Ball "fatally bland" and not believable as a 19th century Milanese soldier.

Our critic's own review of the show said, "The production seems a little self-conscious, frequently seeking your approval or acceptance. It asks for laughs, for applause and, most of all, for feeling. Broadway was bolder. Somehow it didn't give a damn about what other people thought. Like Fosca, it pandered to no one.

"Undoubtedly, those who approach life as Fosca recommends, with 'no expectations,' should enjoy this production. But those of us who have grown to value the demands of Sondheim's subtlety may find [producer] Bill Kenwright's *Passion* at times just a little too blatant."

The review seemed to me to be strong but hardly offensive. The reviewer had similarly assessed the London productions of *Company* and *A Little Night Music*.

To my surprise, Sondheim didn't wait to write. He called. He was incensed and he started right in. I tried to respond but he kept interrupting.

- How could we print this? (It was a good, balanced review.)

- You didn't quote the other reviews accurately. (It cited positive phrases and negative ones.)

- They were "wildly enthusiastic." (Audiences might have been, but that wasn't true of all the critics.)

- This review wasn't fair. (It was balanced and fair.)

- Had the critic even seen the show in New York? (Yes, twice, leaving the theater "in tears.")

- [Our writer] doesn't have any credentials to write about musical theater. (The critic was the drama director for a national theater and also an assistant director of an opera company.)

- Our writer didn't understand what *Passion* was about. (The writer had loved *Passion* in New York and had written notes about it. These were shared with the show's London director, Jeremy Sams, and they met "for three or four hours." Sams had incorporated many of our writer's thoughts, especially a greater sense of Giorgio's conversion.)

I didn't have a chance to explain *TSR*'s position and Sondheim finally hung up. I was baffled. This wasn't the Stephen Sondheim who had been so encouraging and helpful to me and *The Sondheim Review* for the last couple of years. We had published strong reviews by critics of other shows without complaints. Why was this one so upsetting?

I couldn't believe that he was actually ranting—and that's the only word for it. It reminded me of the times at *The Milwaukee Journal* when I had to defend a reporter's story against an angry source, except that those callers didn't get personal about the reporter.

I immediately wrote Sondheim a letter, saying all the things I wasn't able to say on the phone. I defended our critic and pointed out that among London's daily newspapers, there were six negative reviews and three positive, and among the Sunday reviews, there were three positive and two negative. I said I didn't think the London critics were misrepresented in the review and offered to send him copies.

Sondheim received my letter after he wrote his to *TSR*. He apologized for his behavior on the phone but not for what he had said.

May 1, 1996

Dear Paul –

My apologies for getting so upset over the phone, but, as one of your readers pointed out, XXXXX gives falsified reports, according to the way XXXXX feels.

Actually, Sondheim had misquoted a letter printed in the same issue as the *Passion* review. That letter called our writer's reviews of the London productions of *Company* and *A Little Night Music* "calculatedly tepid and quite failed to convey the elation which both of these shows generate."

The letter had not "pointed out" that the reviews were "falsified," as Sondheim said. That would have been libelous. And I wondered how Sondheim knew how our writer "feels."

What's also strange about the whole episode is that after the paragraph attacking our critic, Sondheim moved on to tell a humorous story about *Forum* as if the *Passion* review didn't matter.

One small addition for your next issue, if you wish: in the interview with Nathan, he speculated that Milton Berle decided that Forum *"wasn't funny enough" so he backed out. The fact is that the script he was handed was four hours long. When George Abbott suggested mildly that perhaps we should cut one and a half hours, we did, and Milton got upset because the cuts included some of his lines. He also wanted to play the drag scene in the second act instead of Hysterium. We parted company.*

And, again, he signed it "Best, Steve."

I wrote to him again, defending our writer's reviews and added: "I want the Review to be able to express all sorts of opinions about your work, prompting discussions and debates. Certainly your work invites that kind of discernment. But I also want the reviews, and the responses, to be fair, accurate, and informed."

Sondheim did not reply to this letter, but he called again. Although he was not as heated as on the first phone call, he made the same points. He berated the reviewer and said *TSR* should not have run the review. Again, he didn't listen to my explanations and he finally hung up.

I tried writing again:

"Well, I must confess that I am baffled. I don't mean to be dense, but I would really like to know *why* you think XXXXX's review of *Passion* is unfair. Please give me reasons."

He did not reply in writing or, thankfully, by phone. And he never mentioned the review again.

We published the paragraph about Milton Berle in our Summer 1996 issue but not Sondheim's attack on our critic. It would have been ethically and legally irresponsible to print a libelous statement.

Writing about this episode twenty-five years later, I am still baffled and have no explanation.

A few months later, he responded to the Summer 1996 issue. In it, we had reported that the George School in Newtown, Pennsylvania, from which he graduated at 16, had given him a distinguished alumnus award. It was at the school that he and two other students had written a musical called *By George* which contained such songs as "I'll Meet You at the Doughnut," "Puppy Love," and "Study Hall Dirge." We also published a long profile/interview with Jonathan Tunick, the orchestrator for nearly all of Sondheim's works. Sondheim's letter contained a little praise and a request.

July 25, 1996

Dear Paul –

Department of Amplification anent the Summer issue:

By George was not a "boy-meets-girl situation," but a local school satire, which accounts for the odd titles for what you call the "less-than-memorable" songs.

In the interview with Jonathan Tunick, he's too modest to say why I asked him to score Company. *When I saw* How Do You Do? I Love You,

I thought I was listening to an orchestra of twenty-five. I was astounded when I glanced in the pit and saw that Jonathan had made the sound with an orchestra half that size. There has never been anybody like him in theater orchestration.

Otherwise, the issue seems accurate (and good).

Best,

Steve

P.S. I see you're giving a prize of my crossword puzzle book to the solver of the crossword. Do you have any extra copies? I've been trying to locate them for years.

SS

"Stephen Sondheim's Crossword Puzzles" were so rare that Sondheim had to ask me for copies? Some necessary background: Sondheim, who had a lifelong addiction to games and puzzles, devised a series of "cryptic puzzles" in the late 1960s for *New York Magazine*. These, he explained, were puzzles that offered cryptic clues rather than bald definitions. Several dozen puzzles were collected in a spiral-bound booklet in 1980, but it had long been out of print. I found a copy and published a puzzle in each of our one-year anniversary issues. They had such names as "Vicious Circles," "Chessman," "Woodbabes," and "Printer's Devilry." We usually offered a CD or a rare poster as a prize for a winning entry, but one year I gave away the booklet itself. So I had to turn Sondheim's request down. "If I get more," I wrote him, "I will certainly forward them to you."

$Q \& Q$ WITH SONDHEIM

I N SPITE OF the confrontation over the London *Passion* review, Sondheim the following November readily answered a series of questions we had forwarded from readers. He seemed eager to do so, writing in corrections and additions to the copy before sending it by fax and suggesting that I call him in Connecticut if I had questions. These are the questions and answers, including his changes and additions, which we printed in the Winter 1997 issue.

TSR: Given your interest in education, would you consider accepting a writer/composer-in-residence position at a university in America?

SS: Accepting a writer/composer position strikes me as a fantasy. How many students in how many colleges are interested in the specific craft and discipline that I practice? Very few, I suspect, and certainly among those who are interested in the specifics not a lot who want to go into professional careers, and not a lot who are both skilled or able to be skilled and who are also dedicated and have a voice.

Compounding the problem, of course, would be the fact that it takes a good deal of, at least for me, isolation and uninterrupted time to write and I don't think that kind of teaching position would be conducive to getting my work done. The advantage of Oxford was that I went over for one- or two-week concentrated periods and then came back to the United States for a month or three weeks at a time and therefore had the opportunity to write and do my own work in between stints of teaching and concentrating on the students' work.

TSR: Do you ever yearn to write in other forms—absolute music?

SS: I've always been equally interested in theater and music, and therefore never considered writing concert music. I did write a few instrumental pieces in college and while studying with Milton Babbitt, but those were in the interest of exercise rather than performance. Although, in fact, a violin...I called it a sonata at the time when I was 20 years old, but it was more like a sonata-form suite for solo violin—is going to be performed shortly by Christina Prince, a professional violinist who is Charles Prince's wife, Charles being Hal Prince's son. She found out from me that the piece existed and wanted to play it, and so it will be performed in a couple of small venues over the next few months.

My other so-called concert pieces consist of a couple of piano suites, three movements of a two-piano concerto, and a piano sonata that I wrote as part of getting my degree. They're all, except for one of the piano suites and a couple of movements of the two-piano pieces, pretty academic.

TSR: Would any of your songs serve as your epitaph?

SS: Not a whole song, but my first reaction would be the line from "Our Time" in *Merrily,* "There's so much stuff to sing." Sorry if that sounds overly sentimental, but there it is.

TSR: Of all your works, which one finally met your original vision best? Why?

64

SS: Except for *Sweeney Todd* and *Passion*, the works were never my vision. They were the visions of the librettists. In the case of *Sweeney Todd*, of course, it was Christopher Bond's vision, but it wasn't for a musical. I just saw the play and wanted to make it into one. And in the case of *Passion*, it was not even a novel. It was Scola's movie, and that's what made me want to make it into a musical. And in those two cases—*Passion* and *Sweeney Todd*—I started to write *Sweeney Todd* on my own and asked Hugh Wheeler to help, and on *Passion*, of course, I went to Jim Lapine right away.

I suppose it's also possible to say that *Into the Woods* grew out of a desire of mine to do a fairy tale of some sort, and Jim had the idea of combining a number of fairy tales; it then became his version of my vision.

So the answer as to which one finally met my vision best, of the two under discussion, certainly *Passion* was closer to what I'd imagined, though in fact I didn't have any particular vision of it. I'm not primarily a visual thinker. In the case of *Sweeney Todd*, it was exactly the reverse. Hal's idea was entirely opposite to mine. I had conceived of it as a small chamber melodrama, and he latched on to it as a large-scale melodrama, almost Dickensian in scope, resonating from the industrial revolution and the social setup that resulted in England in the first half of the 19th century. It was a much more political view than I ever had.

As for the vision of the others, you'd have to ask the librettists.

TSR: Would you consider a concert version of *Saturday Night*?
SS: *Saturday Night* is an awfully light-hearted score; I don't think it would hold up particularly well in a concert. It might, though, since a lot of light-hearted scores are doing that these days. But there is a small

move afoot: the Bridewell Theater in London, which is a tiny theater that takes great pride in doing offbeat work in musical theater, gave sort of a little concert presentation of *Saturday Night* earlier this year.

And they would like to do it as a piece, and so maybe we will. It held up very well, considering it's very much of its period. But a concert version—I would rather just do a record.

TSR: You were "someone in a tree" for *Allegro*, a distinct departure from the usual book musical. Do you think the fact that you were close to this show influenced your interest in moving in different, and new, directions with each of your own shows?

SS: I didn't realize how much *Allegro* had in fact had an influence on me until I gave a small introduction to a concert version of it that was done at City Center in 1994.

I emphasized how experimental the form is even though the language and dialogue are traditional, in fact old-fashioned. But Oscar was an unrecognized avant-gardist in form, unrecognized because the style in which he chose to write and his sensibilities were not as sophisticated as the forms.

But in getting close to the show again, I realized how important and far-reaching was his desire to experiment with the fluidity of the stage; the cinematic techniques that *Allegro* pioneered were then used by the more successful *South Pacific*, and of course that influenced all shows afterward. I hadn't realized how much my own sensibility was affected by being close to that piece.

Follies ANNIVERSARY

O UR FALL 1996 issue celebrated the 25th anniversary of *Follies* and naturally I wanted to make this extra special. I obtained Van Williams' exquisite photos for a spread inside and Martha Swope's color photograph of Alexis Smith (Phyllis) for the cover. Smith and Dorothy Collins (Sally) weren't with us anymore, but we had nice interviews with Gene Nelson (Buddy, shortly before he died), John McMartin (Ben), and Yvonne De Carlo (Carlotta).

Reached by phone, Nelson said, "Stephen Sondheim's greatest contribution [to theater], besides his interesting and difficult melodies, is his way with words.

"*Follies* had a very complicated subplot. I was absolutely amazed during rehearsals that whenever I felt lost with my character, I could just go back and read the lyrics. He's the only songwriter I've ever known who defines a character so completely, more so than the writer or the director ever could. Whenever I got into trouble, I'd just read Buddy's lyrics, and say, 'Oh, there he is!'

"It's amazing how Steve gets inside the guts of the characters and exposes their weaknesses and foibles. He's incredible, one of the greatest lyricists ever. I think his lyrics are the strongest part of his talent. There are other, better tune writers, but having said that, the thing is that he makes the tunes fit the lyrics. It's not, 'Oh, here's a tune, I think I'll put some lyrics to it.' No, no. First, he gets into the character, then he writes the words, then—and this is my opinion, but I'm sure this is how he works—he might have a melody in his mind at the same time, but basically, I think the melodies accommodate the lyrics. It's really lovely stuff."

We asked McMartin about "Live, Laugh, Love," which was written in Boston.

"I had a different number, more of a 'dandy' kind of a song. But Steve and I would go out for a drink—he wanted to get to know you. And I think in this particular case, the song grew out of whatever I was telling him as an actor, the interpretation.

"There's a part in it where Ben goes up [forgets his lines], and when we were in Boston, actors were coming up from New York and they'd say, 'That's one of the scariest moments,' because they know it can happen. But some people thought I really was going up. In fact, I think one of the critics said that McMartin would be all right as soon as he gets his lines down. I said to Hal, 'Hal, they think that that's me going up.' 'And he said, 'Yes!'"

De Carlo was also happy to talk about "I'm Still Here."

"Stephen Sondheim had written a very complicated number for me—'Can That Boy Fox Trot'—and I got through it…all right. We even recorded it with an orchestra. But it just wasn't right, and I also felt it wasn't the right number for me.

"So Sondheim decided to write something a little more fitting to my personality as sort of a vamp—a femme fatale sort of thing. He wrote another one, especially for me, about someone who's endured through the years and keeps going—'I'm Still Here.' And now, when all the other actresses do it, I get jealous, and I yell out into the air, 'That's my song! You can't do my song, Carol Burnett!'"

She laughed as she referred to the highly praised 1985 *Follies in Concert* recording, but was blunt in her evaluation of Burnett's performance:

"Her interpretation is not as good as mine. I love Carol Burnett, but when she treads on my territory…" and she paused, still laughing at her own possessiveness, "more than that, I cannot say!"

ON THE FOLLIES *Score*

ALSO IN THE FALL 1996 issue, we were pleased to publish a Q&A about the score between Sondheim and Scott Ross, a playwright in Raleigh, N.C. Here it is in its entirety.

Scott Ross: *Follies* opened to a drum-roll—"soft tympani, like thunder from a long time ago," as James Goldman described it in the published script. The Winter Garden curtain rose on the deserted stage of the crumbling Weisman Theatre. A showgirl appeared, spectral and impossibly tall. She slowly began to move, and the stage came to life as figures from past and present commingled to the strains of an ethereal waltz—guests and ghosts together—participants in a show-biz reunion unlike any ever seen. Who came up with the visuals, with using the concept of the ghosts and the instrumental [a song from *The Girls Upstairs* called "All Things Bright and Beautiful"]? Theater lore had it that the final opening was the brainchild of the show's choreographer and co-director Michael Bennett. Had the collaborators always intended the show to begin this way?

Stephen Sondheim: There was one other version. Our opening as outlined in the script, Michael Bennett staged. What we had wanted was a collage of sound—old songs and sounds. And when we opened in Boston, it seemed to confuse the audience. We had a conference, and Michael said we had to clarify what the opening represented, instead of it being a collage of sounds and old songs, He said, "Let me hear all the songs you cut from the show."

"All Things Bright and Beautiful" was from the original, in which the women performed a kind of Follies. In the rehearsal for this Follies number, Ben—who was still deluded about his romance with Sally—bought her a bouquet of flowers, and Sally had a fugue in the middle of the number. She went up the staircase to Zeigfeld's office and the others—Ben, Phyllis, and Buddy—followed her up the stairs. This was before we got the show to Hal Prince. So, I played that tune for Michael, which he'd never heard.

SR: When did the show begin to evolve from *The Girls Upstairs* to *Follies*? Before Prince came in, or after?

SS: It's the same show, essentially, just under a different title. Hal said, "*The Girls Upstairs* sounds too much like whores."

SR: It was said at the time of the 1971 production that the final script for *Follies* was the twenty-fifth draft. Which draft had Prince read?

SS: Hal read the eleventh draft. The numbers are misleading, because James writes two working drafts for every full draft—eleven full drafts being twenty-two drafts over a period of four years.

SR: Would you discuss "The World Is Full of Boys," one of the cuts that ended up in *Stavisky*?

SS: "The World Is Full of Boys" was in the original surreal Follies sequence. It was a duet between Phyllis and Ben—a kind of "Anything You Can Do, I Can Do Better" number. He was talking about chorus girls, and she was saying, "I can do anything you can do…" I had already written "Losing My Mind" for both Phyllis and Sally. It was supposed to have been like an old MGM musical number, even up to the chorus boys all dressed alike and looking like Ben. Then Alexis asked for a dance number, so we gave "Losing My Mind" to Sally, and I wrote "Uptown, Downtown" for Phyllis. [Note: the song was later replaced by "The Story of Lucy and Jessie."] Because of that, we decided not to have "Losing My Mind" as a chorus number, since we'd just had one. Bob Avian staged that number, by the way, not Michael. That's for collectors of trivia. Originally, I was going to have Sally do a solo number in a swing over the audience. We didn't decide how to do the Follies sequence until we were actually in rehearsal, except for "Losing My Mind," which I had already written.

SR: After the Cameron MacIntosh-produced revival of *Follies* opened in London in 1987, you told the BBC talk show host Terry Wogan that the London show was "different in texture" from the original Broadway production. A *London Times* critic referred to it as more "reassuring" than its progenitor, in which Sally really had seemed actually to have lost her mind at the end of the show. How did this softening of *Follies'* previous, harder edges come about?

SS: That was Cameron MacIntosh. James [Goldman] had never liked the ending we went with before and Cameron thought it was just too down. I disagreed, but since James agreed with him, I didn't want to stand in the way. Why not do it differently? How often do you get a chance to do a production of *Follies*? It's [the new ending's] not soft. It's more hopeful. Also, Mike Ockrent's physical production was more realistic, Hal's was less so, in terms of sets. Hal's notion of the

surrealism all evening long is what gave it its texture. First of all, James'
writing is not realistic by nature. It's stylized. I always thought that
notion of ending with one couple having high hopes and one couple
having lower hopes was a good one.

SR: Between its original Broadway production, the concert recording, and the London incarnation, *Follies* appears to have evolved more
than any other Sondheim show aside from *Merrily We Roll Along*.
During the London production, Cameron MacIntosh quoted you as
not considering the show a revival, but rather "treating the show as an
entirely fresh production." Can you comment on the distinction?

SS: No, they're not comparable at all. We revised *Follies* in London
at the request of Cameron MacIntosh. I don't want that version performed, ever [again]. So this is not an evolution, it's more trying a different version. With *Merrily*, George and I have been working on it for
years.

SR: If revived today, in an ideal production (and an ideal world, in
which money was no object), which version would you prefer?

SS: The original.

SR: For the London production, Ben's Follies number "Live Laugh
Love" was dropped and replaced by a new, and rather different, number
called "Make the Most of Your Music." What was the reason for this
change?

SS: Cameron MacIntosh felt the original ending was too down. I
like "Live Laugh Love" a lot, but since I'd agreed to try...If you'd seen
the staging, it would have made sense to you. The whole point was Ben

was climbing the keys of this enormous piano that Maria Bjornson designed—a "Stairway to Paradise" idea. And when he hit the highest note at the top of the piano keys, Sally exploded out of the piano to join him, and Buddy followed, checking up on Sally, with Phyllis after him. The piano was dropped in by four stagehands, and since they couldn't get it off stage after the number, the young couples came in and sang. I didn't like it, but there didn't seem any way around it. The problem with the whole Follies sequence originally was getting all four of the principal characters into it. The piano idea was a way of making it more obviously the breakdown of all of them, rather than, seemingly, of just Ben—even though they all four go into the Follies. The song doesn't say, "I don't care." It just says, "I do the best that I can."

SR: *Follies* is, among other things, about the lure—and the lie—of nostalgia. Now, however, the show seems—however unintentionally—almost to have become a piece of nostalgia itself. Was the London production more "nostalgic"? Or are people—especially critics—unable to see the use of extravagant, out-sized sets as a part of the whole concept of the show?

SS: If you're trying to show the mistake of living in the past, you have to show the past. That's the reason for all the old-style numbers.

SR: James Goldman's work on *Follies* is still being knocked; the *Times* critic wrote that the musical was "a wonderful idea for a show which has failed to grow into a story." It seems to me that the form of Goldman's book is perfect for the style and content of *Follies*. It isn't a "book" show, and incident is far less important to the show than atmosphere.

SS: Book writers always get it in the neck. The ones I've worked with, with one or two exceptions, have been terrific. Except for *West Side Story*, it's the most compact of any musical libretto. Everyone talks in highly stylized dialogue. If you have characters who speak realistically, you can't have a surrealistic show surrounding them.

SR: I recently had a conversation with a friend, a theater director, who had been to the Winter Garden in 1971. He told me that he'd never seen a show as moving as *Follies* in 1971, and has never seen anything as moving since.

SS: I've seen other shows that moved me more. But it was certainly an extraordinary show visually, and one that had to be seen at least twice, because it was so rich.

SOME "*Juvenilia*"

AVING FOUND interesting early work by Sondheim on *Forum* at the Wisconsin Center for Film and Theater Research, I returned to Madison to look at work from his high school and after-college years. I wrote a piece about a couple of rarities for the Spring 1997 issue.

One was a musical that Sondheim co-wrote in the 1940s when he was a student at the George School in Newtown, Pennsylvania. Based on the legend *The Lady or the Tiger*, in which a courtier must choose which door a princess or a tiger is behind, the talky sixty-five page script included a dozen songs.

This is a portion of a song the king sings about his daughter—remember this was written by a high school student:

I'm proud of my castle,
My golden throne
Gives me justified pride,
Each underpaid vassal
Whose soul I own
Makes me glad inside.
But more than my riches
And jewels and such
Is my daughter to me.
And nothing bewitches
Me half so much
Or so well as she.

Sondheim went back to the story in 1954 with his friend Mary Rodgers, the daughter of Richard Rodgers, for a proposed television musical. This was at a time when TV musicals were popular—*Our Town, High Tor, One Touch of Venus, High Button Shoes, Peter Pan,* and so on—and Mary Rodgers was to return to the same genre later with *Once Upon a Mattress.*

Only a few pieces of this *Lady* were on file in the archives: lyrics for four songs, music for five, a twenty-one-page outline, and the first seven pages of the script. I found this fascinating and asked Sondheim why it wasn't completed. He said it was a little show "written for ourselves," not on speculation or contract with a network or producer.

"I guess we lost interest in it," he said. "Or we didn't know how to sell it."

We reprinted portions of several songs, including one as a soft shoe dance for a character accused of deserting twenty-seven wives:

Each time that I've been tried
I've picked myself a bride;
My brides are high and wide
And handsome.
They're gay and fancy-free,
So free they're costing me
A king's ransom,
And then some!

Another song foreshadowed "Somewhere" in *West Side Story*:
There has to be another world,
Another place for us to start.
We'll meet again, and yet

With curious rapport,
We'll wonder where we've met
Before.
There has to be another world,
Another haven for the heart,
Another time to be
When this time is through,
Another chance for me
To love you!

Even though Sondheim had answered my questions about the work with Mary Rodgers, he was not pleased that *TSR* had written about the two *Lady* versions.

April 23, 1997

Dear Paul –

The issue looks fine, but I must say that I object vigorously to your reprinting my juvenilia. Not only is it embarrassing, but I feel you are nibbling me to death. No more, please. Stick to the published work. Granted, my reaction is exacerbated by the fact that you tend to leave out the most important parts of the lyrics when you quote them. For example, the refrain line of "Once I Had a Friend": For some peculiar reason, you quoted the entire verse and not the important part of the chorus, thereby killing the final quatrain.

The lead article in that issue was a report on "A Conversation with Stephen Sondheim" that took place at Trinity College in Hartford, Conn., on March 9 of 1997. Sondheim and a Trinity professor discussed music and casting. Sondheim responded to the article:

A couple of corrections and elucidations: [The author of the article] mistakes the word "harmonics" for "harmonies" in his paragraph about Gypsy. *Violin "harmonies" are meaningless in context. And Professor XXXXX's question about non-traditional casting ignores the fact that the cast of* Pacific Overtures *was composed entirely of Asian-Americans. I didn't bring this up at the time because I didn't want to embarrass him.*

Otherwise, everything seems kosher.

Best,

Steve

We also reported on developments on the Mizner brothers musical, which had assumed the name *Wise Guys*. John Weidman said he was writing the second act but still working on the first. Sondheim said he had finished the opening number and was writing the second. The show was now commissioned by the Kennedy Center in Washington, and a reading was scheduled in February 1997, a workshop in late spring, and a full production in the fall of 1997.

Also in 1997, a film called *Broadway Damage* was released. On *Rotten Tomatoes*, it gets an approval rating of 29 percent, but that didn't matter to me. It included a brief sequence in which a character walks up to a New York newsstand, picks up a copy of the Summer 1995 issue of *The Sondheim Review* (the one with Sondheim, Bernadette Peters, and Madeline Kahn on the cover) and starts to read it until he is diverted. That was our two minutes of cinematic fame.

MORE *Letters*

T HE SUMMER 1997 issue included an interview with long-time Sondheim pianist Paul Ford; an examination of the extended scenes in Sondheim musicals that amounted to one-act plays; and essays on the music and lyrics for *Saturday Night*. We also contacted Arte Johnson, who remembered his role in the backers' audition for *Saturday*. After reading the issue, Sondheim corrected Johnson's memory.

July 24, 1997

Dear Paul –

The new issue looks swell, and I particularly enjoyed XXXXX's exegesis on Saturday Night *(although you might tell him that the opening figure in "All for You" is a rising sixth, not a fifth).*

In the department of more important corrections, Arte Johnson's memory is a little hazy. First of all, he couldn't have come out to California to meet with Phil Epstein, since the latter had been dead for a number of years. He must mean Julie [Julius]. Also, Hal Prince and George Abbott had nothing to do with the show—Arte was chosen for the auditions by Lemuel Ayers. And the audition was not in Lem's living room but in the spectacular pseudo-aviary (here Arte's memory is accurate) of Mr. and Mrs. Osborn Elliott (who, interestingly enough, were the models for the couple in John Guare's

Six Degrees of Separation—*the basic incident of the play actually happened to them.)*

An additional piece of information, in case anybody's interested (and you may have printed it already): Arte left the cast after the first four auditions and was replaced by Joel Grey.

Best,

Steve

Our Fall 1997 issue included a letter from a reader who said:

"I really want to like Stephen Sondheim. A true musical genius, he is one of the great composers of the 20th century. But Mr. Sondheim persists in giving such cranky responses to each issue of *The Sondheim Review,* a publication in which the reviews and essays regarding his work are consistently positive and flattering. He invariably locates one trivial error which he makes the centerpiece of his comments, and then follows that with a briefer explication of one or two additional 'mistakes' uncovered elsewhere in the issue. After two paragraphs of criticism in the Summer 1997 issue, the closest Sondheim seems to get to a positive comment is, 'Otherwise, everything seems kosher.' His comments have a tone of exasperated irritation."

On October 16, 1997, Sondheim sent me a letter addressed "To the Editor."

XXXXX seems to think that my corrections to each issue of the Review are "cranky responses." I assure him they are not. They are corrections and nothing more, and I offer them in the interest of accuracy, knowing that the care and authenticity of the articles and reports in the magazine will be used as the basis of future "scholarship" about the shows.

Yours sincerely,
Stephen Sondheim

In the envelope was another letter.

October 16, 1997
Dear Paul –
A couple of corrections to the Fall issue.

Julius Epstein is not the "co-author" of the book of Saturday Night, *but sole author. The confusion arises because he and his brother Philip were co-authors of the book* Front Porch in Flatbush, *from which the musical was derived.*

The reprise of "Have I Got A Girl For You" was performed at the Donmar. In fact, it was Sam Mendes's idea—he needed something to substitute for "Tick-Tock" as a scene change.

Best,
Steve

We published both letters in the next issue.

Saturday Night OPENS

I N THE FALL OF 1997, the tiny (133-seat) Bridewell Theater in London announced that it would host the world premiere of *Saturday Night*, the show Sondheim wrote in 1955 but was never produced. This, of course, was a major event in the Sondheim world, and I went over to cover its December 17 opening.

As I reported in the Winter 1998 issue, "It was surely the most improbable world premiere a Stephen Sondheim show has had. No bright lights or limousines. No showbiz types filling the theater. In fact, since this was also press night, the audience was more scruffy than celebrity."

Perhaps I should have noted that the Bridwell was located just off of Fleet Street.

In my comments about the production, I said *Saturday Night* was worth being resurrected because it "reveals some of the lyric and musical innovations that would mark Sondheim's later work," that it could play off-Broadway or in a small regional theater, and that it should be recorded, preferably with the Bridewell cast.

I said I thought the story of a group of boys trying to get a date on Saturday night in Brooklyn had a conventional book, was very much of its time, was too long, was sometimes sexist, and should have been funnier.

I also had some thoughts about the songs:

"In '*Saturday Night*,' Sondheim showed how an opening song could set the scene for the entire show.

"'Class' has class written all over it. Its harmonic shifts and the feel of it are very advanced for 1955.

"'Love's a Bond,' crooned by a Rudy Vallee-like bandleader, lent just the right touch to the Plaza Hotel scene.

"'In the Movies' is one of Sondheim's funniest songs: *"If a person treads the path of sin/So her daughter can eat quail/In the movies she's a heroine,/But in Brooklyn she'd go to jail."*

"'A Moment with You' is not only a brilliant example of Sondheim pastiche but also the show's sprightliest song.

"When Anna Francolini started to sing 'So Many People,' you could almost hear the gasps of recognition. The most famous song from the show, because of numerous recordings, here it was a duet for Helen and Gene.

"'I Remember That,' the duet for Celeste and Hank as they recall their first date differently, is a nice turn for the supporting characters.

"The lovely 'All for You' is too fragile to follow the big confrontation scene."

The London critics recognized that this was an early Sondheim work but that it forecast what was to come.

The Times said, "Catching snatches of the later Sondheim in the twists of the music and the dapper rhymes is certainly fun….The occasion is gently pleasant, but one can see why Sondheim was content to turn his attention elsewhere all those years ago."

The Guardian's comments: "Astonishing to find a Sondheim musical getting its world premiere in a disused swimming bath off Fleet Street….No one, least of all Sondheim himself, would claim that

From the Pages of *The Sondheim Review:*
A SMALL SELECTION

The Sondheim Review

Vol. 2 No. 1   *Dedicated to the Work of the Musical Theater's Foremost Composer and Lyricist*   Summer 1995

EXPANDED 1ST ANNIVERSARY ISSUE

- Scott Ellis on *Company*

- *Follies* revived

- *Whistle* in concert

SONDHEIM ON VIDEO BY KEN MANDELBAUM

$5.95

Madeline Kahn, Stephen Sondheim and Bernadette Peters after the
Anyone Can Whistle concert in 1995. Photo by Donna Aceto.

An early Hirschfeld drawing.

Stephen Sondheim at Fairfield
University in 2000.
Photo by Susan Warner.

STEPHEN SONDHEIM

April 26, 1984

Dear Paul Salsini -

Thanks for the lovely letter. It
helps the ego no end, and at a time when
ego-building is of the essence.

Enjoy the enclosed.

Yours,

Stephen Sondheim

*P.S. The rest consists of Arte Johnson,
Jack Cassidy, Alice Ghostley,
Leila Martin, Jay Harnick, Robin
Oliver and Richard Kallman.*

At the recording session for *Passion*: Sondheim, Steve Murphy, James Lapine,
Tony MacAnany, Phil Ramone, producer. Photo by Joan Marcus.

SONDHEIM & Me

The Sondheim Review

Vol. 1 No. 1   *Dedicated to the Musical Theater's Foremost Composer and Lyricist*   Summer 1994

Premiere Issue

- Sondheim on *Passion*

- *Merrily Rolls Along*

- *Evening Primrose*

$5.95

The first issue of *The Sondheim Review*.
Jere Shea and Donna Murphy in *Passion*. Photo by Joan Marcus.

Andrea Ascari as Robert in
Company in Bologna 2000.

STEPHEN SONDHEIM

May 13, 1994

To the subscribers everywhere -

I'm flattered and embarrassed and delighted
at your interest. I can only hope there will be
enough news to justify publication.

Thanks for the support.

Happily,

Stephen Sondheim

Sondheim's note in the premiere
issue of *The Sondheim Review*,
Summer 1994.

SONDHEIM & Me

Stephen Sondheim wrote both the music and lyrics for a show called *All That Glitters* while a student at Williams College.

presents
THE CAP AND BELLS, INC.
Production of

ALL THAT GLITTERS

(Based on the GEORGE S. KAUFMAN—MARC CONNELLY play
"BEGGAR ON HORSEBACK")

$

Book, Lyrics and Music by
STEPHEN SONDHEIM
Production under the direction of
DAVID C. BRYANT
Costumes and Scenery by
O. W. SIEBERT
Choreography by
IDA KAY

...SIC INC. • 580 FIFTH AVE. • NEW YORK 19, N.Y.

The Minneapolis Musical Theatre's production of *Sunday in the Park with George* featured Christopher Zenner as Georges and Stacey Lindell as Dot in 2003. Photo by Roy Blakey.

Deborah Hope obviously did not want to get married today in *Company* at Houston's Stages Rep in 2000. Photo by Bruce Bennett.

Larry Kert and Susan Browning in the original production of *Company* in 1970.
Photo by Zodiac Photographers.

Sondheim answering questions from students at the Booker T. Washington High School
in Dallas 1994. Photo by Richard Micheal Pruitt/The Dallas Morning News.

Brian Stokes Mitchell as Sweeney and Christine Baranski as Mrs. Lovett in the Kennedy Center's *Sweeney Todd* in 2002. Photo: Joan Marcus.

STEPHEN SONDHEIM

May 5, 1994

Dear Paul –

Thanks for the sweatshirt -- I love those things, although wearing it in New York will seem a bit like self-advertising. But it will be terrific in the country.

Best,

The Sondheim Review

Vol. 2 No. 2   *Dedicated to the Work of the Musical Theater's Foremost Composer and Lyricist*   Fall 1995

COMPANY'S BACK ON BROADWAY

- The '70 cast reminisces
- Sondheim and Furth
- New mystery also opens

$5.95

$7.95 Canada

0 74470 86580 3

Boyd Gaines as Robert and Jane Krakowski as April in the Roundabout Theater's revival of *Company* in 1995. Photo by Carol Rosegg.

Patricia Levy was Suzi and Claudio Botehlo was Robert in *Company*. Rio de Janeiro 2001. Photo by Chico Lima.

STEPHEN SONDHEIM

November 6, 1986

Dear Mr. Salsini -

What a lovely gesture! Thank you. I think I will wait a bit to listen to the tape, at least until I finish the score to <u>Into The Woods</u>. Shocks are not good for my nervous system.

Yours gratefully,

Stephen Sondheim

Ben (Daniel Massey) in the London production of *Follies* in 1987. Photo by Michael Le Poer Trench.

Donna Murphy as Fosca in *Passion*. Photo by Joan Marcus.

The Sondheim Review

Vol. II No. 4   *Dedicated to the Work of the Musical Theater's Foremost Composer and Lyricist*   Spring 1996

- *Murder* dies quickly
- Patinkin on *Sunday*
- Sondheim parodies

NATHAN LANE STARS IN *FORUM*

$5.95

Nathan Lane and Leigh Zimmerman in the revival of
A Funny Thing Happened on the Way to the Forum in 1996. Photo by Joan Marcus.

Jan Schepens as Robert in *Company*,
Amsterdam 1995. Photo by Luk Monsaert.

John McMartin was The Narrator in the 2002
revival of *Into the Woods*. Photo by Joan Marcus.

LEMUEL AYERS and JOHN B. RYAN III

present

AN AUDITION OF

"SATURDAY NIGHT"

•

Book by JULIUS J. EPSTEIN & PHILIP G. EPSTEIN

Music and Lyrics by STEPHEN SONDHEIM

At the piano: MR. SONDHEIM

Assistant to MR. SONDHEIM, Joe Lewis

Those attending the backers'
audition for Sondheim's first
Broadway show, *Saturday
Night* in 1955, were given
this program.

Giorgio (Jere Shea) and Clara (Marin Mazzie) find one another
"So Beautiful" in *Passion*. Photo by Joan Marcus.

STEPHEN SONDHEIM

March 18, 1988

Dear Mr. Salsini -

Thanks so much for your letter -- it made me feel wonderful.

Gratefully,

Stephen Sondheim

Stephen Sondheim.
Photo by Joe Marzullo.

Laurence Paxton was Georges and Yvonne Filius was Dot in the 1994 production of *Sunday in the Park with George* in Honolulu.

Lynn Redgrave as Joanne in the Kennedy Center's *Company* in 2002. Photo by Joan Marcus.

The Kennedy Center in Washington announced its Sondheim Celebration in 2002 with an ad listing the shows to be presented.

The Sondheim Review

Vol. IX No. 2   Dedicated to the Work of the Musical Theater's Foremost Composer and Lyricist   Fall 2002

- Q&A with Sondheim
- *Woods* settles in
- *Overtures* in N.Y., D.C.

KENNEDY CENTER FESTIVAL A HUGE SUCCESS

$5.95

Michael Hayden as Franklin, Miriam Shor as Mary and Raul Esparza as Charley in the Kennedy Center's production of *Merrily We Roll Along* in 2002. Photo by Joan Marcus.

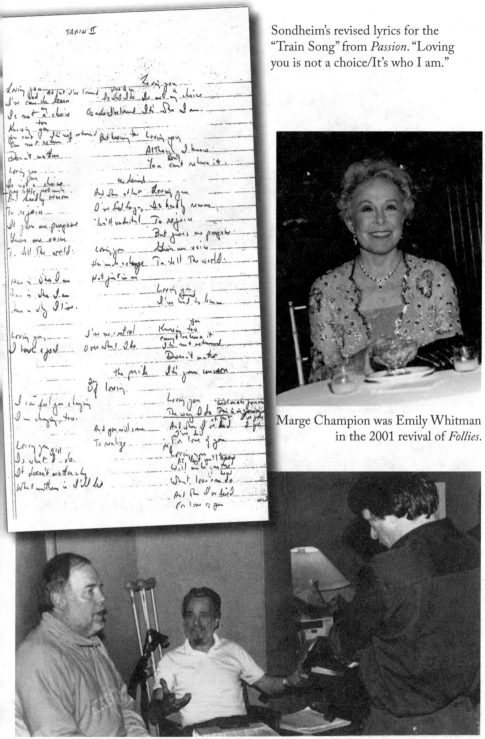

Sondheim's revised lyrics for the "Train Song" from *Passion*. "Loving you is not a choice/It's who I am."

Marge Champion was Emily Whitman in the 2001 revival of *Follies*.

Music Director Paul Gemignani, Stephen Sondheim and RCA Victor Executive Producer Jay David Saks at the recording session for *Assassins*.

Stephen Sondheim.
Photo by Michael Le Poer Trench.

STEPHEN SONDHEIM

May 3, 1991

Dear Paul Salsini -
    Thanks a million for the review -- you're
absolutely right. Mr. Adler is the only critic
who picked up on the Rapunzel story being the
springboard of the entire piece.

            With thanks,

            Stephen Sondheim

Masaki Kosuzu as Manjiro and Shuji Honda as Kayama in the New National Theater's *Pacific Overtures* in Washington, D.C., in 2002. Photo by Stephanie Berger.

Jere Sjea as Giorgio in *Passion*.
Photo by Joan Marcus.

Joan Roberts was Heidi Schiller in the 2001 revival of *Follies*. Photo by A. Tedesco.

SONDHEIM & Me

The Sondheim Review

Vol. III No. 2   *Dedicated to the Work of the Musical Theater's Foremost Composer and Lyricist*   Fall 1996

- *Passion* on PBS

- Gemignani on Sondheim

- Exploring *Stavisky*

CELEBRATING *FOLLIES'* 25ᵀᴴ ANNIVERSARY

$5.95

Alexis Smith as Phyllis in the original cast of *Follies*.
Photo by Martha Swope © Time Inc.

Terry Mierau was the Balladeer in *Assassins* in Montreal 1996.

MAY 22'95   11:09 No.002 P.02

e of Hits

STEPHEN SONDHEIM

May 18, 1995

Dear Paul -

In answer to your questions:

There's nothing further to be said about the Mizner musical. We're busily writing it.

I'm also in the process of rewriting the murder mystery, which is now called The Doctor Is Out.

I don't know what Scott means about having more "hands-on" participation in the Company revival than for the Night Music revival, but perhaps he means that we may be (and I emphasize the word may) adding some material that was not in the original.

I don't think they've cast a replacement for Ian McKellan. The reason he's not doing it is that he's been trying for a long time to raise money for a film of "Richard III" and finally has the financing in place and so will be filming it over the next few months.

The things destroyed in the fire were all my reference books and a lot of vocal scores and CDs. None of the personal papers, but all my sheet music (by other composers). And of course my dog Max died.

That's about it. You probably know more about my activities than I do.

Best,

Matt Yoder as Lee Harvey Oswald, Sherri Z. Heller as Sara Jane Moore and Sean Young as John Wilkes Booth in *Assassins* in Ephrata, Penn., in 2000. Photo by George Winchell.

SONDHEIM & Me

Sondheim answering questions from students at Southern Methodist University in November 1994. Photo by Carol T. Powers/Dallas Morning News.

STEPHEN SONDHEIM

July 25, 1991

Dear Paul Salsini -

Thanks for the letter, but I fear I must
disappoint you. Though Finney's Rainbow and
All That Glitters may have been moderately
sophisticated for a college undergraduate, they're
not something I would like to expose publicly.
Please forgive me.

As for the Assassins album, it will be released
in a couple of weeks, and it's terrific. I'm glad
you liked the show -- me, too.

Apologetically,

Stephen Sondheim

Seth Teter was Henrik and Kris Koop was Anne in *A Little Night Music* in Westport County, Conn., in 1995. Photo by Jason Byrd.

PAUL SALSINI

The Sondheim Review

Vol. VI No. 3   *Dedicated to the Work of the Musical Theater's Foremost Composer and Lyricist*   Winter 2000

Wise Guys is canceled

- Preparing *Saturday Night*
- *Waltz* in New Jersey
- Translating Sondheim

PUTTING IT TOGETHER OPENS ON BROADWAY

$5.95

Carol Burnett in *Putting It Together* in New York in 1999.
Photo by Michael Le Poer Trench.

SONDHEIM & Me

Amy Jane as Sara Jane Moore and Johanna Schloss as "Squeaky" Fromme in *Assassins* in St. Louis 1994.

Stephen Watts as the Proprietor in *Assassins* at the New End Theater in London, 1997. Photo by Ash Scott Lockyer.

STEPHEN SONDHEIM

May 1, 1996

Dear Paul -

My apologies for getting so upset over the phone but, as one of your readers pointed out, Ms. Davies gives falsified reports, accor▮▮▮▮▮ way she feels.

One small addition for your next issue, if you wish: in the interview with Nathan, he speculated that Milton Berle decided that *Forum* "wasn't funny enough" so he backed out. The fact is that the script he was handed was four hours long. When George Abbott suggested mildly that perhaps we should cut one and a half hours, we did, and Milton got upset because the cuts included some of his lines. He also wanted to play the drag scene in the second act instead of Hysterium. We parted company.

Best,

Steve

Franc D'Ambrosio as Henrik in a concert version of *A Little Night Music* in San Francisco 1998. Photo by Cary C. Heider.

UNCLE JACK

presents

"BY GEORGE"

A Musical Comedy
in two acts

Book, Music, and Lyrics
by
Miriam Dubin, James Lincoln, and Steve Sondheim

starring

Art Henrie   Cindy Kamp
By Hollinshead   Peggy Weimar
          Margo Rintz

with

Molly Wood   Betsy Zerega   Tedd Ward
Gwen Kerr   June Spackman   Bobbie Forrest
      Midge Metz   Ed Willson

and

the Misses Chalmers, Frazee, Palumbo, Foster, and
Mason as the Women Faculty

PLUS

the Messrs. Fraser, Frescoln, Carson and McMillen
as the "BIG FOUR"

Sondheim and two other students wrote a musical called *By George* when he was a student at the George School in Newtown, Pennsylvania. He called it a school satire.

Miriam Shor as Mary in the Kennedy Center's *Merrily We Roll Along* in 2002. Photo by Joan Marcus.

The Sondheim Review

Vol. VII No. 3   *Dedicated to the Work of the Musical Theater's Foremost Composer and Lyricist*   Winter 2001

- Previewing the new *Follies*
- The director gives details
- Examining *Night Music*

PACIFIC OVERTURES PREMIERES IN JAPAN

$5.95

Masaki Kosuzu as Manjiro and Shuji Honda as Kayama in the Japanese premiere of *Pacific Overtures* in Tokyo in 2000. Photo by Tsukasa Aoki.

Michael Hayden as Franklin Shephard in the Kennedy Center's *Merrily We Roll Along* in 2002. Photo by Joan Marcus.

Glynis Johns from *A Little Night Music* at an AIDS benefit in Hollywood 1996. Photo by Michael Lamont.

Sondheim in a talk at Orchestra Hall in Chicago in 1995. Photo by Mark Dobrzycki.

STEPHEN SONDHEIM

August 7, 1991

Dear Mr. Salsini -

Unfortunately, there's no score of the college shows on file anywhere. Sorry. However, a few of the songs were published and I'm enclosing duplicates of them.

Yours,

Stephen Sondheim

Marin Mazzie as Clara in
Passion. Photo by Joan Marcus.

Sondheim answering
questions at SMU.
Photo by Andy Harson.

Victor Garber arrived for a
rehearsal of a *Wise Guys* workshop.
Photo by Joseph Marzullo.

The Hirschfeld drawing for *A Little Night Music.*

Whitney Allen as Dot and
Adam Hunter as Georges in the
University of Michigan's production
of *Sunday in the Park with George.*
Photo by David Smith.

SONDHEIM & Me

Joel Sutliffe was Georges in Pegasus Players' *Sunday in the Park with George* in Chicago in 2002.

STEPHEN SONDHEIM

August 30, 1993

Dear Paul (we might as well be on a first-name basis) –

I'm delighted that you want to be the "American correspondent for the newsletter" but, as I warned someone over there, there may not be that much news.

As for the American productions of the shows, I rarely know about them till after they're over. I can tell you about the few "professional" ones that I know about as they arise, but I can also put you in touch with someone at Music Theater International, the organization which leases the rights to all the shows except <u>Gypsy</u>. He will know of every forthcoming production, from small town to university to touring, as they all have to apply for licenses from the organization (I have no "publicist").

I won't be in New York on September 10th and 11th, but in Connecticut, working furiously on a new show which starts rehearsals for a workshop two days later. Sorry about that, but if you want to talk, you can call me at (my New York number is , and please don't give either of these numbers out).

Yours,

Steve S.

Bernadette Peters was Dot and Mandy Patinkin was George in the orignal production of *Sunday in the Park with George* in 1984. Photo by Martha Swope.

PAUL SALSINI

The Sondheim Review

Vol. VII No. 4   Dedicated to the Work of the Musical Theater's Foremost Composer and Lyricist   Spring 2001

*Blythe Danner as
Mrs. Phyllis Rogers Stone*

*Gregory Harrison as
Mr. Benjamin Stone*

*Judith Ivey as
Mrs. Sally Durant Plummer*

*Treat Williams as
Mr. Buddy Plummer*

AFTER 30 YEARS, *FOLLIES* IS BACK ON BROADWAY

$5.95
Canada $7.95

Blythe Danner, Gregory Harrison, Judith Ivey and Treat Williams in the
Roundabout Theater's revival of *Follies* in 2001.

Sondheim with a student at SMU. Photo by Any Harson.

Miranda Gas as Fredricka and
Montserrat Carulla as Madame
Armfeldt in *A Little Night Music*.
Barcelona 2000.

When *Saturday Night* premiered in
New York in 2000, David Campbell
was Gene and Lauren Ward was Helen.
Photo by Joan Marcus.

Michael Bennett and Stephen
Sondheim on the opening night
of *Follies*, April 4, 1971.

Charmain Carr and Anthony Perkins
in Sondheim's television special
Evening Primrose, shown in 1966.

Deborah Gibson had the
title role and Betty Buckley
was Mama Rose in *Gypsy*
at the Paper Mill Playhouse
in 1998. Photo by Joan
Marcus.

SONDHEIM & Me

STEPHEN SONDHEIM

July 18, 1994

Dear Paul -

The magazine looks classy and the articles are literate, accurate (for the most part) and not too hagiographic -- congratulations. A few corrections and elucidations, however:

In the piece by ███████ about *Passion* previews, he states that "When Fosca collapses in the storm scene, Giorgio originally stalked off, then returned ". No, originally Giorgio never left the stage. He merely stood in angry resignation downstage left, then crossed upstage to Fosca. James (Lapine) added the stalking off later. As for the change from "ugliness" to "wretchedness", it was not intended to "make Giorgio more sympathetic to Fosca" but to take care of the fact that Donna Murphy, no matter how much prosthesis and makeup we put on her, was never able to look ugly. And the reason for the laugh on "When I die I'll leave you my braids" was that to a modern audience the notion sounds ridiculous, whereas to a 19th Century audience it would have sounded natural -- leaving one's hair to one's lover or family was a common legacy.

Glynis Johns as Desiree and Len Cariou as Fredrik in *A Little Night Music* 1973. Photo by Martha Swope.

In ███████ report on *Merrily We Roll Along*, he makes one (perfectly natural) mistake in assuming that "Not A Day Goes By" was "transferred from Franklin to his first wife, Beth". Actually, it was a reversion -- the song was originally written for Beth to sing, but during previews of the 1981 production it became clear that the girl who played the part simply couldn't manage it so I had to make a quick lyric fix and give it to Jim Walton, who could. It was always meant for Beth, whether or not Mr. Stearns thinks it works. And in the elucidation department, Stearns omits the major change in the show from all previous versions: namely, that we folded Scene 2 (which took place in a restaurant) into Scene 3 (which takes place in a television studio) in order to keep the focus more on Frank and less on Charley and Mary. Seeing this change performed for the first time in Leicester, England, in 1992 is what convinced us that the show was enough improved to make this the definitive version and to let the York Theatre produce it, which I think they did in first-rate fashion.

Congratulations again,

[signature]

Loretta Bailey was Cinderella in the Canadian Stage Company's *Into the Woods* in Toronto in 1995. Photo by Michael Cooper.

The Sondheim Review

Vol. VIII No. 4   *Dedicated to the Work of the Musical Theater's Foremost Composer and Lyricist*   Spring 2002

- The Kennedy Celebration
- *Gold!* suit is settled
- *Assassins* resonates

REVIVAL OF *INTO THE WOODS* OPENS IN L.A.

$5.95

Kerry O'Malley as The Baker's Wife, Stephen deRosa as The Baker and Vanessa Williams as The Witch in the revival of *Into the Woods* in 2002. Photo by Joan Marcus.

Barbara Cook as Sally and Lee Remick as Phyllis in *Follies* in Concert at Lincoln Center in 1985. Photo by Martha Swope.

Barbara Bryne as Jack's Mother and Ben Wright as Jack in the *Into the Woods* tryout in San Diego in 1986. Photo by Peter Weiss.

Kate Baldwin as Clara, Christopher Invar as Giorgio and Maree Johnson as Fosca in *Passion* in Philadelphia in 2001. Photo by George Golem.

Sean Phillips was Madame Armfeldt in *A Little Night Music* in London in 1995. Photo by Mark Douet.

STEPHEN SONDHEIM

January 12, 1996

Dear Paul -

Dept. of Corrections and Emendations:

In reference to the Fall issue, David Shire did more than "new orchestrations" on "Tick Tock" -- he wrote the music. And anent the ending of <u>Company</u> in Boston, Bobby was not sitting on a park bench but by a pool. And he was not approached by a "previously unseen person, a member of the vocal minority," but by Teri Ralston, playing (as did everybody else) a character different from the one she had played during the course of the show. And despite Hal's recollection, the reason the show was cut was that it was a half hour too long.

In the Winter issue, on p. 8 the lyric should read, "It's not talk of God and the <u>moon</u>" (not "mood"). And readers might be interested to know that I went to Barcelona to see the Catalan production of <u>Sweeney Todd</u> that gave rise to the recording mentioned on p. 29, and it was one of the most thrilling experiences I've ever had in the musical theater: full of ferocious energy, over-the-top performances (even the set made the actors look larger than life)

and brilliantly detailed staging (they had three months to rehearse, as opposed to the American five weeks' worth and the British eight).

Keep up the good work.

As always,

Patrick Cassidy, the Balladeer, and Victor Garber, John Wilkes Booth, record "The Ballad of Booth" for the *Assassins* CD.

Kenneth Marshall as Cinderella's Prince, Kim Crosby as Cinderella and Joanna Gleason as the Baker's Wife in the *Into the Woods* tryout in San Diego in 1986. Photo by Peter Weiss.

Leslie Uggams was the Witch in *Into the Woods*, Houston 2001. Photo by Bruce Bennett.

Tammy Grimes appears with Nancy Jacobs in Williamstown Theatre's opening production of *A Little Night Music*. Photo by Richard Feldman.

STEPHEN SONDHEIM

October 19, 1994

Dear Paul –

I enjoyed Issue #2 very much, and even learned some things I didn't know. One erratum: It's <u>Jane</u> Greenwood, not Joan, who designed the costumes for <u>Passion</u>. Joan was a well-known British actress.

See you in November, I expect...

After long delays and revisions, the Sondheim/Weidman musical about the Mizner brothers, now called *Bounce,* would have its world premiere at the Goodman Theater in Chicago in 2003.

Michael Hayden, Raul Esparza and Thursday Farrar (the TV interviewer) in the Kennedy Center's *Merrily We Roll Along* in 2002. Photo by Joan Marcus.

STEPHEN SONDHEIM

January 27, 1995

Dear Paul –
    Sorry to have missed you in New York, but I was up to my neck with the filming of <u>Passion</u> and another project, of which you'll be hearing shortly.

                                Best,

Vanessa Williams as The Witch in the 2002 revival of *Into the Woods*. Photo by Joan Marcus.

PAUL SALSINI

The Sondheim Review

Vol. V No. 1   *Dedicated to the Work of the Musical Theater's Foremost Composer and Lyricist*   Summer 1998

4th Anniversary Issue

- Sondheim in Kansas
- *Follies* cast records CD
- Biography reviewed

CELEBRATING *NIGHT MUSIC'S* 25TH ANNIVERSARY

$5.95

Len Cariou as Fredrik and Glynis Johns as Desiree in the original cast of
A Little Night Music. Photo by Van Williams.

Stephen Sondheim and John Weidman's newest musical— commissioned by the Kennedy Center!

Broadway's greatest composer immortalizes the infamous Mizner brothers, two of the most colorful characters of the Roaring Twenties. Con men, gold rushers, self-promoters, and bon vivants, the Mizners yield a gold mine of material for a brilliant new musical—see it at the Kennedy Center first!
JULY•AUGUST 1997

A Special Workshop Presentation of

WISE GUYS

Book by
John Weidman

Music & Lyrics by
Stephen Sondheim

with

Brooks Ashmanskas Jessica Boevers Candy Buckley
Chamberlin Christopher Fitzgerald Victor Garber Michael Hall
Nathan Lane Jessica Molaskey Nancy Opel William Parry
Clarke Thorell Lauren Ward Ray Wills

...ed by	.Sam Mendes
...graphed by	.Jonathan Butterell
...Director	.Ted Sperling
...Designed by	.Mark Thompson
...es Designed by	.Santo Loquasto
...t Designed by	.Jules Fisher & Peggy Eisenhauer
...esigned by	.Jonathan Deans
...Supervisor	.Paul Gemignani
...tions	.Jonathan Tunick
	.Jim Carnahan
...n Stage Manager	.Bonnie Panson
...Manager	.David Bradford
...ss Representation	.Barlow•Hartman public relations

From the program of the Wise Guys *workshop.*

The Kennedy Center in Washington announced that it had commissioned a new musical by Sondheim and John Weidman called *Wise Guys* and it would be performed in the summer of 1997.

Aki Avni as John Wilkes Booth and Gil Verner as Lee Harvey Oswald in *Assassins* in Tel Aviv in 1998. Photo by Leche Lepid.

The cover of Newsweek on April 23, 1973, two months
after the opening of *A Little Night Music.*

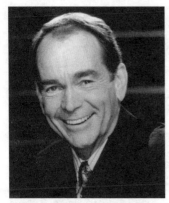

Dean Jones played Robert in the original *Company* in 1970.

Chuck Wagner as Count Carl-Magnus Malcom and Diana Canova as Charlotte Malcom in *A Little Night Music* in 2000 at the North Shore Music Theater. Photo by Paul Lynden.

Scott Ellis, director of the Roundabout Theater's revival of *Company* in 1995.

Jere Shea at the recording session for *Passion*. Photo by Joan Marcus.

STEPHEN SONDHEIM

July 25, 1996

Dear Paul -

Department of Amplification anent the Summer issue:

By George was not a "boy-meets-girl situation," but a local school satire, which accounts for the odd titles for what you call the "less-than-memorable" songs.

In the interview with Jonathan Tunick, he's too modest to say why I asked him to score Company. When I saw How Do You Do? I Love You, I thought I was listening to an orchestra of twenty-five. I was astounded when I glanced in the pit and saw that Jonathan had made the sound with an orchestra half that size. There has never been anybody like him in theater orchestration.

Otherwise, the issue seems accurate (and good).

Best,

P.S. I see you're giving a prize of my crossword puzzle book to the solver of the crossword. Do you have any extra copies? I've been trying to locate them for years.

Pseudolus (Nathan Lane) gives advice to Philia (Jessica Boevers) and Hero (Jim Stanek) in the 1996 revival of *Forum*. Photo by Joan Marcus.

Ruth Williamson as Cora in *Anyone Can Whistle* at Hollywood's Matrix Theater in 2003. Photo by Ed Krieger.

Hal Prince and Sondheim during the production of *Merrily We Roll Along*. Photo by Rivka Shifman Katvan.

SONDHEIM & Me

STEPHEN SONDHEIM

April 23, 1997

Dear Paul -

The issue looks fine, but I must say
that I object vigorously to your reprinting
my juvenilia. Not only is it embarrassing,
but I feel you are nibbling me to death.
No more, please. Stick to the published
work. Granted, my reaction is exacerbated
by the fact that you tend to leave out the
most important parts of the lyrics when you
quote them. For example, the refrain line
of "Once I Had A Friend": For some
peculiar reason, you quoted the entire
verse and not the important part of the
chorus, thereby killing the final quatrain.

A couple of corrections and
elucidations: Mr. Rizzo mistakes the word
"harmonics" f████████ies" in his
paragraph about Gypsy. Violin "harmonies"
are meaningless in context. And Professor
Moshell's question about non-tra██
████████gnores the fact that the cast of
Pacific Overtures was composed entirely of
Asian-Americans. I didn't bring this up at
the time because I didn't want to embarrass
him.

Otherwise, everything seems kosher.

Best,

Sondheim at the Plymouth
Theater on opening night of
Passion. Photo by Bruce Janiga.

The production of *A Little Night Music* by the New York City Opera in 1990.
Photo by Carol Rosegg.

Stephen Sondheim and Carol Burnett at the opening night party for *Putting it Together*. Photo by Joseph Marzullo.

STEPHEN SONDHEIM

July 24, 1997

Dear Paul —

The new issue looks swell, and I particularly enjoyed ███████████ exegesis on <u>Saturday</u> <u>Night</u> (although you might tell him that the opening figure in "All for You" is a rising sixth, not a fifth).

In the department of more important corrections, Arte Johnson's memory is a little hazy. First of all, he couldn't have come out to California to meet with Phil Epstein, since the latter had been dead for a number of years. He must mean Julie (Julius). Also, Hal Prince and George Abbott had nothing to do with the show -- Arte was chosen for the auditions by Lemuel Ayers. And the audition was not in Lem's living room but in the spectacular pseudo-aviary (here Arte's memory is accurate) of Mr. and Mrs. Osborn Elliott (who, interestingly enough, were the models for the couple in John Guare's <u>Six Degrees of Separation</u> -- the basic incident of the play actually happened to them).

An additional piece of information, in case anybody's interested (and you may have printed it already): Arte left the cast after the first four auditions and was replaced by Joel Grey.

Best,

[signature]

Helen Hobson as Clara and Michael Ball as Giorgio in the London production of *Passion* 1996. Photo by Michael Le Poer Trench.

Mary Ellen Mahoney as Countess Charlotte Malcom and Kristin Gauthier as Anne Egerman in *A Little Night Music*. 1996 at the St. Lawrence Centre for the Arts. Photo by Elisabeth Feryn.

SONDHEIM *& Me*

Dave Willetts as Sweeney
Todd in the Haymarket
Theater in London 1996.

Debra Monk as Joanne in the
Company revival. Photo by
Carol Rosegg.

Dee Hoty performs
"Ah, but Underneath"
as Phyllis in *Follies*
at the Paper Mill
Playhouse in 1998.
Photo by Gerry
Goodstein.

The Sondheim Review

Vol. IV No. 3   *Dedicated to the Work of the Musical Theater's Foremost Composer and Lyricist*   Winter 1998

- Sondheim's movie scores
- Anniversary for *Woods*
- L.A. loves Sondheim

SATURDAY NIGHT PREMIERES IN LONDON

$5.95

Anna Francolini as Helen and Sam Newman as Gene in the world premiere of *Saturday Night* at the Bridewell Theater in London in 1997. Photo by Bridget Kimak.

SONDHEIM & Me

STEPHEN SONDHEIM

October 16, 1997

Dear Paul –

A couple of corrections to the fall issue.

Julius Epstein is not "co-author" of the book of <u>Saturday Night</u>, but sole author. The confusion arises because he and his brother Philip were co-authors of the book "Front Porch in Flatbush," from which the musical was derived.

The reprise of "Have I Got A Girl For You" <u>was</u> performed at the Donmar. In fact, it was Sam Mendes's idea -- he needed something to substitute for "Tick-Tock" as a scene change.

I'm genuinely impressed that four of your readers solved the puzzle despite the misprinting.

Best,

To the Editor –

Barry A. Bass seems to think that my corrections to each issue of the Review are "cr███████." I assure him they are not. They are corrections and nothing more, and I offer them in the interest of accuracy, knowing that the care and authenticity of the articles and reports in the magazine will be used as the basis of future "scholarship" about the shows.

Yours sincerely,

Stephen Sondheim

Donna Murphy and Marin Mazzie at the recording session for *Passion* in 1994. Photo by Joan Marcus.

Jim Merlo was Giorgio and Deborah Sharn was Clara in *Passion* at the New Line Theater in St. Louis in 1996.

Russell Dixon was Ben and Mari Gordon-Price was Phyllis in *Follies* at London's Haymarket Theater in 1994.

Again, a challenging puzzle by Sondheim

In what has become a tradition for our anniversary issue, *The Sondheim Review* is pleased to present a puzzle from the long out-of-print *Stephen Sondheim's Crossword Puzzles* (Harper & Row 1980). Again, we warn readers that these are not the familiar kind of puzzle but offer cryptic clues rather than definitions.

This one is entitled Dedicated Dodecahedron, and Sondheim acknowledges "Jeffec of The Listener."

The winner will be chosen at random from among the correct entries received by August 15 and will receive a program and poster from the acclaimed production of *Pacific Overtures* by the New National Theater in Tokyo in 2000. The production will play at the Kennedy Center in Washington, D.C., as part of its Sondheim celebration in 2002.

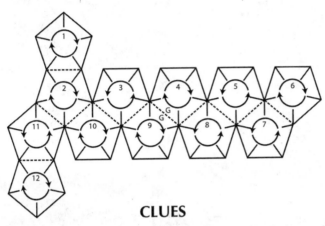

CLUES

Group A: 6-letter words
1. Madden with wild anger—to a point
2. Traffic Commissioner sounds out buildings on the farm
3. Obituary for a Box Office? When it's able, it's healthy
4. Attired—and often with interest
5. Mixtures of completely Yiddish sighs?
6. Bad radio—end of broadcast is skillful
7. Moocher is a scoundrel—in short, German
8. Little Islands take it less badly
9. Without starting, looks fleetingly at spears
10. Stick fast at this place
11. He makes you laugh a nasty laugh about a Saint
12. Scotch? Boy, tot it up and fib about it

Group B: 5-letter words
1. Pigpens are sites for sore eyes
2. Ox Guide
3. I had started, but stopped working
4. Naughty Lola's jars
5. Society girl and party inside are back, as predicted
6. The Terrible Irene, Queen of France
7. There's a horse inside—does it taste edible?
8. Princess? Kelly green begins the competition
9. Yes, yes, I'm eager—in a way
10. Suffers saber moves
11. One dart thrown in three
12. Wash dirt out of the auricle and ventricle

Instructions: The diagram would form a regular twelve-sided solid if folded along the dotted lines.

The clues in group A lead to words of six letters; each of these words contains all the (mixed) letters of a five-letter word plus one extra letter. The five-letter words are clued in group B. The extra letters are to be entered in the centers of the appropriate pentagons with the associated five-letter words inscribed around them (to read in the direction shown by the arrows) in such a way that, *at each edge of the solid, adjacent letters are the same.*

When the diagram is complete, the central letters from 1 to 12 will spell the name of the person to whom the puzzle is dedicated.

N.B. The clues are in no particular order; the answer to clue #1 in group A is not necessarily associated with the five-letter answer to clue #1 in group B. The solver must figure out which answers are "associated" with each other and where to place them.

Example: The answer to a clue in group A might be *warden*; the answer to a clue in group B might be *drawn*. Since *warden* contains the letters in *drawn* these two words would be "associated" and *drawn* would be entered (in the direction of the arrows) in a pentagon, surrounding the extra letter E, in such a way that the D, the R, the A, the W, and the N would each be duplicated in another word on the adjacent side of an edge.

All answers are words in English, except for two common foreign words and one surname.

One letter, with its duplication, has been printed to help you get started.

Ignore punctuation, which is designed to confuse.

On its one-year anniversaries, *The Sondheim Review* published a cryptic puzzle that Sondheim had created for New York Magazine. This one was called "Dedicated Dodecahedron."

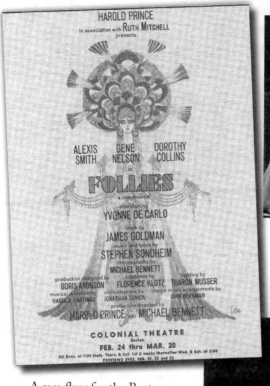

Ruth Cracknell was Madame Armfeldt and Andrea McEwan was Fredricka in *A Little Night Music* in Melbourne, Australia in 1996.

A rare flyer for the Boston tryout of *Follies* in 1971. John McMartin had not yet been cast as Ben.

Stephen Sondheim referring to *Saturday Night*.

TO: Mr. Paul Salsini

December 15, 1997

Dear Paul -
    I thought the book was charming and the score promising.

Marie Danvers as April and Davis Gaines as Robert in the Huntington Theater Company's production of *Company* in 1997. Photo by T. Charles Eriksen.

The Sondheim Review

Vol. IX No. 1   *Dedicated to the Work of the Musical Theater's Foremost Composer and Lyricist*   Summer 2002

8TH ANNIVERSARY ISSUE

- A Sondheim talk in D.C.
- *Woods* opens on Broadway
- A journal by 'Rapunzel'

KENNEDY CENTER BEGINS SONDHEIM CELEBRATION

$5.95

Alice Ripley as Amy in the Kennedy Center's production of *Company* in 2002.
Photo by Joan Marcus.

In a gender switch, Zachary Hallie (center) was Marty, not Martha, in Pittsburgh's Carnegie Mellon University's *Company* in 2002. Annika Bob was Kathee and Jacqueline Baker was April. Photo by Joshua Fonzos.

STEPHEN SONDHEIM

January 3, 1995

Dear Paul –

The new issue looks very good indeed. Congratulations again. A few small corrections, however:

Shevelove's name is Burt, not Bert.

I didn't go with Jerry Robbins to the gang dance -- he merely reported on it.

And it's true that I made up the Beggar Woman's slang to begin with, but I then found a British source for authentic cockney, and changed the lyric.

More important, Bob Mondello's report on the liner notes for the British <u>Merrily We Roll Along</u> is unfortunate. The notes are almost ludicrously incorrect, as is Mr. Mondello's report that Mary (!) is the iodine-thrower. I █████████ agree with his assessment of the recording, but the irony is that the cast in Leicester was wonderful. The problem lies with the r███████ who is notorious for doing shows that nobody else is recording (which is good) but on the cheap (which

- 2 -

is bad). One of the results of the latter is that he was so anxious to rush the long-delayed recording into release that he didn't let me vet the liner notes. I've asked Mark Shenton, the writer, to correct the numerous errors, if there ever should be a reprinting. Meanwhile, tell your readers not to pay any attention to the notes whatsoever -- including the "historical" ones.

To satisfy my own curiosity, I'd love to know where Frank Rich's quotes about █████████ from.

Again, in spite of these things, congratulations. Happy New Year to all of us.

Tom Wopat as Sweeney Todd and Barbara Marineau as Mrs. Lovett in Augusta, Michigan in 1995.

Noam Talmon as Robert and Sharon Yefet as April in the Israeli production of *Company* in 1995.

February 27, 1998

Dear Paul -

Brief answers to brief questions:

Yes, we certainly will allow <u>Saturday Night</u> to be performed elsewhere. We'll cut some of the book, which we never had a chance to in the past because we not only never had a production but not even a reading of the show until the Bridewell. MTI does indeed want to include it in their catalogue. The tape of the record sounds very good to me, although a couple of tempos are a little off. The band was indeed augmented, although not by much -- the orchestrations are by Peter Corrigan. There were no changes in the songs or cast. I don't know if the Bridewell will get any official credit in subsequent productions, but they will certainly get credit in any interviews I give or any publicity.

We hope to have a reading of the complete <u>Wise Guys</u> in May and a production in Washington next February. At the moment we're working on a few revisions in the first act; the score is still only half done.

There are no new developments on <u>Assassins</u> as far as I know. John has written about a third of the script, and it's terrific.

Yes, the information I said you could have for this issue concerns the L.A. production of <u>Putting It Together</u>, which will star Carol Burnett, and which will have a number of changes in it. I'm still planning them, so I can't tell you exactly what they will be. Suffice it to say that we want to tailor this version for Carol.

Nothing else new on the creative front. If you want to fill out the Review, you can tell the folks that I'm receiving an award at the William Inge Festival, an annual event held in Independence, Kansas, on April 19th. The last recipients were August Wilson and Neil Simon. Bernadette and Elaine Stritch will attend and perform, along with others, and I'll have a seminar or two with some students.

Best,

[signature]

P.S. No comment on the Winter Issue. It was fine. SS

Sal Viviano was George and Liz Larsen was Dot in *Sunday in the Park with George* at Arena Stage in 1997. Photo by Joan Marcus.

The Sondheim Review

Vol. IX No. 4   *Dedicated to the Work of the Musical Theater's Foremost Composer and Lyricist*   Spring 2003

- *Gypsy* on Broadway
- *Night Music* at City Opera
- *Gold!* is now *Bounce*

A NOSTALGIC *FOLLIES* IN CONCERT IN MICHIGAN

$5.95

Kurt Peterson, Virginia Sandifur, Harvey Evans and Marti Rolph in a concert of *Follies* in Ann Arbor, Michigan, in 2002. Photo by Julie Peterson.

Sondheim wrote the music and co-wrote the book and lyrics with a fellow student for *Phinney's Rainbow* while at Williams College.

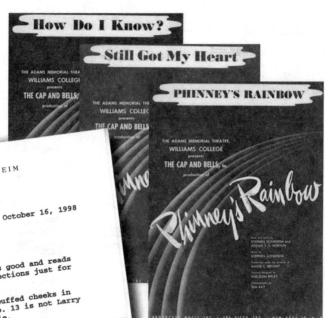

STEPHEN SONDHEIM

October 16, 1998

Dear Paul –

The new issue looks good and reads well. A couple of corrections just for the record:

The man with the puffed cheeks in the bottom picture on p. 13 is not Larry Blyden, but Michael Vale.

In the article on Michael Starobin, William Goldman is given credit for "Evening Primrose." As you know, it should be James.

████████ is mistaken when he says that I was working on Do I Hear A Waltz? when I wrote my version of "Do I Hear A Waltz?" I wrote that two years previously for a television musical called "Do You Hear A Waltz?" (not based on The Time of the Cuckoo) – a show that Arthur Laurents and I were going to write but never did.

Best,

Bernadette Peters starred as The Witch in the orginal prodcution of *Into the Woods*. Photo by Martha Swope.

Teach me how to whistle

Anyone can whistle,
Let themselves go
Everyone says — That's what they say
Easy

Everybody whistles

Maybe if you whistle,
Showing me how —
Maybe thought if you would
Maybe if you whistle,
Whistle for me,
Whistle me near
Now. Here and now.
Then Maybe I could whistle here and now.

Relax, let go, let fly —
So someone tell me why
Can't I?

I can dance a tango
I can read Greek
Easy.
I can slay a dragon
Any old week
Easy.
What's hard seems is simple
What's natural seems is hard
Maybe you could show me
How to let go,
Lower my guard,
Learn to be free —
Maybe if you'd whistle,
Whistle for me.

Portions of a draft for the title
song in *Anyone Can Whistle*. It
is included in the Sondheim
collection at the Wisconsin
Center for Film and Theater
Research in Madison.

I can slay a dragon
learn a lesson   I have learned my lesson
play piano   Many a time   too many times
dance a tango
read speak Italian
carve a turkey   Its too natural
name the playbills
weave a carpet
write a sonnet   Even in the shower
turn a cartwheel
Anything that's taught (learneth)   That you can't learn
I can learn   Can't be taught

Timothy Nolen was Sweeney Todd at the Goodspeed Opera House in East Haddam, Connecticut in 1996. Photo by Diane Sobolewski.

Follies was featured on the cover of Time Magazine on May 3, 1971.

Jane Krakowski, Charlotte d'Amboise, and La Chanze in *Company*. Photo by Carol Rosegg.

Russell Dixon as Fredrik Egerman and Kathryn Evans as Desiree Armfeldt in *A Little Night Music* at the Leicester Haymarket Theater in 2001.

STEPHEN SONDHEIM

March 16, 2000

Dear Paul –
    I wish you had let me know about the Service – I'd love to have been there. Did anyone by any chance make a recording?
    Thanks for the birthday wishes, and for the continued dedication.

As always,

Elaine Strich

The Sondheim Review

Vol. X No. 1   *Dedicated to the Work of the Musical Theater's Foremost Composer and Lyricist*   Summer 2003

9th Anniversary Issue

- *Bounce* in Chicago
- *Follies* at Signature
- *Overtures* on tour

BERNADETTE PETERS STARS IN *GYPSY* REVIVAL

$5.95

Bernadette Peters as Mama Rose in a revival of *Gypsy* in 2003. Photo by Joan Marcus.

SONDHEIM & Me

The Sondheim revue *Marry Me a Little* was performed at the Gaslight Club in Chicago in 1987.

Nikkieli Lewis was the Balladeer in *Assassins* in Cincinnati, Ohio in 1997. Photo by Sandy Underwood.

Marry me a little

Songs by
STEPHEN
SONDHEIM

Performances Thurs. 8:00, Fri. 8:00,
Sat. 6:30 and 9:30, Sun. 3:00.
For tickets and information call 641-2923.

Cocktails served (no minimum).   Club membership not required.
Dinner/Theatre packages available. Children under thirteen not admitted.

GASLIGHT CLUB
at the Palmer House, 17 E. Monroe

David Canary was Sweeney Todd and Karen Morrow was Mrs. Lovett in *Sweeney Todd* in 1994 at the North Shore Music Theater. Photo by Richard Fieldman.

The Sondheim Review

Vol. X No. 3   *Dedicated to the Work of the Musical Theater's Foremost Composer and Lyricist*   Winter 2004

- Previewing *Overtures*
- The strippers revealed
- The making of *Follies*

BOUNCE IS IN LIMBO AFTER PLAYING D.C.

$5.95

Richard Kind as Addison Mizner and Gavin Creel as Hollis Bessemer in *Bounce* in Washington, D.C., in 2003. Photo by Liz Lauren.

What do you do with a woman?
How do you know where to start?
I say hello to a woman and fall apart.
What do you do with a woman?
What do you say to a woman?

A portion of the lyrics Sondheim wrote for Hero in an early draft of *A Funny Thing Happened on the Way to the Forum*. Along with many others, the song was abandoned.

A star-studded New York gala in 1992 resulted in the publication of *The Poetry of Song: Five Tributes to Stephen Sondheim.*

The Poetry of Song

Five Tributes to Stephen Sondheim

Robert Creeley
John Hollander
J.D. McClatchy
Grace Schulman
Richard Wilbur

Raul Esparza and Stephen Sondheim at the Sondheim Celebration concert party at Avery Fisher Hall in New York. October 21, 2002. Photo by Karla Merrifield/Star File.

Stephen Sondheim

Saturday Night is a major work. But it has charm, freshness, and wit, and it counters heedless pre-Depression innocence with a tart lyric irony."

The Sunday Independent: "I can see why Sondheim held back. It's a slight piece—a sort of *Friends* in period flocks—about a group of 1920s Brooklyn housemates looking for love. Much of the music is standard '50s Broadway, with no distinctive Sondheim number until a love duet, 'So Many People,' near the end of Act One. But the shape of Sondheim's melody—the scooping-upward leaps and angular descents—is embryonically apparent."

In the United States, *USA Today* said: "Modest, conventional, and hobbled somewhat by libretto problems, *Saturday Night* is still a charmer, and it holds up better than many hits from the mid-'50s...It'll never be more than a specialty piece, but it could make audiences happy in productions as intimate, fresh, and full of the kind of care taken by the young Bridewell cast."

We asked Sondheim, who also attended the premiere, what he thought, and he sent a fax: "I thought the book was charming and the score promising."

It was our cover story. There were other pieces and photos inside, along with articles on Sondheim's work in films and on the way his lyrics could dazzle without drawing attention away from the characters.

I faxed various questions to Sondheim when I returned and he replied by fax on February 27, 1998.

Dear Paul –

"Yes, we certainly will allow Saturday Night *to be performed else-where. We'll cut some of the book, which we never had a chance to do in the*

past because we not only never had a production but not even a reading of the show until the Bridewell. MTI does indeed want to include it in their catalogue. The tape of the record sounds very good to me, although a couple of tempos are a little off. The band was indeed augmented, although not by much—the orchestrations are by Peter Corrigan. There were no changes in the songs or cast. I don't know if the Bridewell will get any official credit in subsequent productions, but they will certainly get credit in any interviews I give or any publicity.

"We hope to have a reading of the complete Wise Guys *in May and a production in Washington next February. At the moment, we're working on a few revisions in the first act; the score is still only half done.*

"There are no new developments on Assassins *as far as I know. John has written about a third of the script, and it's terrific.*

[Editor's Note: Sondheim and John Weidman were making some revisions on *Assassins* since its off-Broadway opening in 1990. The same actor would play both the Balladeer and Lee Harvey Oswald, and the song "Something Just Broke" would be added. A Broadway production was planned.]

"Yes, the information I said you could have for this issue concerns the L.A. production of Putting It Together, *which will star Carol Burnett, and which will have a number of changes to it. I'm still planning them, so I can't tell you exactly what they will be. Suffice it to say that we want to tailor this version for Carol.*

"Nothing else new on the creative front. If you want to fill out the Review, *you can tell the folks that I'm receiving an award at the William Inge Festival, an annual event held in Independence, Kansas, on April 19th.*

The last recipients were August Wilson and Neil Simon. Bernadette and Elaine Stritch will attend and perform, along with others, and I'll have a seminar or two with some students.

"That's all. You probably know more about my life than I do."

Best,

Steve

P.S. No comment on the Winter issue. It was fine. S.S.

Having observed all the iterations for *Wise Guys*, I made what I thought was a brilliant proposal to Sondheim. How about a *Wise Guys* journal?

"Either I or a staff member would contact you and Weidman regularly to get an update on what has been done since the last contact. An example: You are writing a song for the two brothers that confronts some conflict between them. How do you approach the song? How do you decide on the musical phrasing? And other questions like that. Our readers are most interested in this show, and I know they would follow this journal very carefully."

Sondheim declined by fax two days later:

January 27, 1998

Dear Paul –

I'm sorry to disappoint you, but I think it's not a good idea. I already feel nibbled at enough, and this would be like undressing in public—or getting dressed. A little mystery is always sexier.

Please forgive me.

As ever,

Steve

Instead, we ran a chronology of the show's various incarnations since Sondheim first thought of the idea in 1952.

PUTTING IT *Together*

THE COVER STORY of our Fall 1998 issue was on the Carol Burnett *Putting It Together* that Sondheim had mentioned in his fax, and we interviewed the director and star before the Los Angeles tryout.

Eric Schaeffer, the director, said that the new effort would not be the same as the 1993 production that played at the Manhattan Theater Club and starred Julie Andrews.

"We're really approaching it like a revue," Schaeffer said. "Each song has to stand on its own. The biggest thing we want to do is make Steve's words and music just sing. That's our first priority. So it gives it a new twist. It's really like rediscovering these songs again, which is really kind of exciting."

For her part, Burnett said she was thrilled to be working with Schaeffer and to be back in Los Angeles doing Sondheim. She starred in *Company* with Patrick Cassidy there in 1993.

She said that Sondheim had sent her tons of materials and CDs and scores, "and he said, 'Write down some of the songs you think you'd like to sing,' which was really nice. I told him I'd want him to pick them out, but that I did want to keep 'Could I Leave You?' and that I would try 'Getting Married Today.' I'll attempt it!

"And I said anything else you want to take out or put in, blow in my ear and I'll follow you anywhere."

The revisions may not have worked well. Our Los Angeles reviewer wrote this for the following issue: "In deciding to accentuate the revue aspect of the show at the expense of characters and storyline, however thin, Schaeffer succeeded in spotlighting Sondheim's work. But without characters to care about singing the songs (and there is still enough of a story here to refer to 'characters' vs. performers, as in a straightforward revue), he also lost some of the music's heart."

Variety added: "Though the show has been substantially revised since its Oxford, England, premiere and subsequent Off-Broadway production in 1993, it still doesn't work. The material comes from no fewer than 11 musicals, one movie, and an unproduced TV special.... All of the songs, however, seem to be forced fits."

Reviews were similar when *Putting It Together* opened on Broadway on November 21, 1999. *The New York Times'* was typical:

"While there are moments in the production, directed by Eric D. Schaeffer, when the Burnett and Sondheim sensibilities coalesce in shiver-making flashes, they are sadly infrequent. The whole tone of the show, which strings together Sondheim songs to shape a loose story of five urbanites at a cocktail party, is out of sync with its own material. *Putting It Together* is perversely determined to make something lite of the dark bard of the American musical....Indeed, the composer's full presence is oddly absent throughout this evening devoted to his work."

The show closed after 101 performances.

SONDHEIM & *Television*

I N NEW YORK, the Museum of TV & Radio's "Something for Everyone: Sondheim Tonight!" screening series included a half hour of video clips and an appearance by Sondheim. *TSR*'s associate editor Sean Patrick Flahaven transcribed the videotape of the program and the following are excerpts.

ON ACTORS' CONTRIBUTIONS:

Performers enrich songs. I'll give you a couple of examples. I had originally written the role of George in *Sunday in the Park with George* as a bass-baritone and Dot as a soprano. Mandy Patinkin insisted on auditioning, and we loved him. And we eventually offered the role of Dot to Bernadette Peters. So we ended up with a tenor and a mezzo. Dot ended up with more warmth and George with more fervor, which you can see in the close-ups of Mandy.

Angela Lansbury in *Sweeney Todd* is an expert comedienne and her performance is almost too big for the screen—it's theatrically gauged. It's rare that a performer really surprises me, but they raise the level. When Merle Louise auditioned for the part of the Beggar Woman in *Sweeney Todd*, she instinctively played up the sexuality of the character, rather than the insecurity, which gave it a whole new dimension.

ON THE TV SPECIAL *EVENING PRIMROSE*:

Evening Primrose was shot in just a couple of days, and we had only one Sunday in Stern's department store. I spent most of the time looking over the cameraman's shoulder. When Tony Perkins asked where he should look while he sang, I told him not to look directly into the lens, but just to the left and right of it. It was terrible advice and as a consequence, he looks cross-eyed. That was the last time I tried to direct anything. [Laughter.]

ON WRITING FOR THE TV SERIES *TOPPER*:

I needed a job. I lived for two years after college with my father and his family on money from the Hutchinson Prize for composition that I had received. I wanted my own apartment. Donald Clopfer, a publisher, put me in touch with George Oppenheimer from MGM, who was looking for an assistant. I had written a couple of TV scripts on spec. I went to California for five months until I had enough money for a New York apartment. George and I alternated writing the scripts. It taught me economy of writing in the four-act, twenty-two-and-a-half-minute structure. It's a rigid framework like a sonnet or a lyric. Arthur Laurents said he learned playwriting structure by writing radio scripts during World War II.

ON HIS ACTING IN THE TV SPECIAL *JUNE MOON*:

I did *June Moon* as a favor to Burt Shevelove. He needed someone who could deliver wisecracks and play the piano. I think I'm the only person who can't get a laugh out of a George F. Kaufman line—I kept inflecting all my sentences down. [He demonstrates. Laughter.] Also, I was having trouble finding my character, so I had lunch with Hal

Prince, and he said, "Wear a hat, all the time, even indoors." So I did—that was my character. There's a real scene I'm in near the end that's pretty good.

ON VIDEOTAPES OF LIVE PERFORMANCES:

They're second best. There's an ephemeral, unique experience in one night of live theater, a feeling that they're performing just for you. But I do approve of the Lincoln Center Archives, which tapes shows for posterity. It's a wonderful resource. I asked some theater people in London why they don't do that, and they were appalled at the idea—as if it would take the soul away from the performance.

ON CHANGING KEYS AND TEMPOS
FOR PERFORMERS:

Keys, yes. Tempos, no. You don't know who will do it when you write a song. In opera, you can believe an overweight, forty-year-old woman can be Juliet, but not in musical theater. You have to adjust for range. Angela Lansbury couldn't handle the big tessitura I had originally written for Mrs. Lovett. In *West Side Story*, Tony was originally supposed to sing a high C. All the tenors who auditioned could hit the note, but they were too old. Lenny [Bernstein] would say [of each one], "He's perfect!" [Laughter.]

ON CHANGING THINGS IN FRONT OF
AN AUDIENCE DURING PREVIEWS:

I learned to make adjustments from watching Oscar [Hammerstein] on *Allegro*. If a song is too long, cut it. They cut "Boys and Girls Like You and Me," which was supposed to be the big hit, from *Oklahoma!*

He was ruthless in adherence to the show. I love changing things in front of the final collaborator, which is the audience. More than one show has closed out of town because the authors refused to make cuts.

ON A DIRECTOR'S CONTRIBUTIONS:

Hal [Prince] approaches things from a socio-cultural perspective—he can't get interested otherwise. He wanted the class structure in *Sweeney Todd*—I wanted to write a horror show. [Laughter.] In a collaboration, if you ask the authors what the theme of the show is, you may get three different answers. You all have to be writing the same show, though. With the exception of *Pacific Overtures*, you'd get different answers from me and Hal about our shows. His strength is a sense of *mise-en-scene*—a visual arc. [James] Lapine's strengths are character, detail, and visual poetry.

ON THE DEMANDS OF HIS REPUTATION:

Fans: Don't expect too much. [Laughter.] I'm worried that I'll let them down, but it's not my fault. [Laughter.]

ON THE DIFFICULTY OF HIS MUSIC:

Some people think my songs are difficult to learn, but if you ask actors who've done them, they'll tell you that they're not that difficult. Paul Gemignani, who has conducted most of my shows, is wonderful in instilling confidence in non-singers. Barbara Bryne was trembling at her audition for *Sunday in the Park with George*, but Paul gave her confidence. When I work with singers, I try to do the same.

ON HAVING HIS SHOWS VIDEOTAPED:

I never go asking for them to be taped. They come to me and tell me. It would have been wonderful if *Assassins* had been taped for PBS. But at the time, we expected it to transfer to Broadway, but that fell through, so there was no chance.

ON THE DIFFERENCE BETWEEN LONDON AND BROADWAY PRODUCTIONS OF HIS WORK:

Into the Woods is the best example because it [the London production] differed most from the New York production. Richard Jones is a wild man—the set was a room with seven doors and the woods on the wallpaper. In the second act, he used a giant eye and finger for the giant. It was truly wonderful and surreal. *Into the Woods* invites the director to interpret. Sam Mendes' *Company* also used the notion of everything in the same room. The Donmar Warehouse has no fly or wing space, so Bobby's apartment doubled as Bobby's mind. *Sunday in the Park with George* at the National was too elaborate, but Declan Donellan did a brilliant *Sweeney Todd* at the National. It was intimate and scary, with almost no scenery. Mike Ockrent did *Follies* realistically in London, and it was written to be artificial, so it wasn't as good.

ON THE QUALITY OF AUDIENCES:

Two generations of people who grew up on TV and pop/rock have gone by, so they're out of the theater-going habit. It's an "occasion" now—whatever the hot ticket is for the middle-aged and rich. They don't talk about the show afterwards. Ask them about it and they'll say, "We had wonderful seats!" [Laughter.] Every show now gets a standing ovation, but I think if you're really moved, you don't stand. They want to remind themselves that it's an occasion—they're applauding themselves. The TV audience only wants to sit down front and have it paraded in front of them. When Hal and I were young and used to go to the theater, we'd sit in the balcony, where you had to lean forward and focus on the show, so your suspension of disbelief was complete. It's less true off-Broadway, where the houses are smaller.

ON BEING THE SAVIOR OF MUSICAL THEATER:

I failed. [Laughter.] Young writers aren't getting the chance to be produced. It takes two years to write a show and forever to get it on. Rodgers and Hart wrote two shows per season. Talents don't get honed now. You can't learn from workshops—you need a paying audience of strangers. That and the state of audiences are why I'm pessimistic now. Theater won't die, but more of it will become a solely commercial venture. Hal and I used to say we got in just under the wire, and we used to complain that it took two years to get a show up!

ON OPERA VERSUS MUSICAL THEATER:

I'm interested in storytelling, not in the human voice itself, just conveying emotion and story. I think operas are too long—individual incidents take too long. Also, I don't want to write opera because there's no chance to fix it with only six performances and a varying cast and orchestra. Beverly Sills once asked me to write an opera, and I asked if she would give me two weeks of uninterrupted performances with the same cast. There was silence. [Laughter.] It isn't done that way—opera audiences want the shows in repertory. John Harbison just had his *Great Gatsby* done at the Met, so now he has a chance to fix it, but the next performance isn't until 2003!

Musicals aren't rewritten—they're written with an audience. *Sweeney Todd* is not an opera, it's an operetta, and was done at City Opera because they do operettas well. Their audience isn't concerned with stars. It wouldn't work in a big Metropolitan Opera production. The Lyric Opera in Chicago also does opera well, because it's more of a theater than an opera house. *Pacific Overtures* shouldn't be done in an opera house, as we discovered in England.

Night Music
ANNIVERSARY

THE SUMMER 1998 ISSUE of *The Sondheim Review* celebrated the 25th anniversary of *A Little Night Music*. Like the *Follies* anniversary, it was our cover story, with a picture spread and interviews with the stars. We asked them about their most famous songs from the show.

Over tea at a Los Angeles hotel, her voice still raspy, Glynis Johns remembered when she first heard "Send in the Clowns." It became both her signature song and Sondheim's most popular piece.

Johns and co-star Len Cariou had been rehearsing a pivotal, emotional scene between former lovers Desiree and Fredrik near the end of the musical. Hugh Wheeler, who wrote the book, had rewritten the scene, but not much had changed. Len Cariou had gone to lunch while Johns, Wheeler, and director Hal Prince sat on the floor discussing what to do next. Prince suggested that Johns explain how she felt about Desiree and what the woman would be feeling at the time. And Johns did so.

"The explanation made sense to Hugh," she said, "and it hit the button with Hal. So when Len came back from lunch, we very briefly filled him in, and then Hal said, 'Now I'd like you two to play the scene and ad-lib it.' And in the middle of this ad-libbing, Hal said he was going to ring Steve and tell him to get there as soon as possible. This was at 3 p.m. Hal told Steve that he thought he would get an idea about my solo here. Hal instigated that! He had a genius for realizing what Steve needed to see to tip him off.

"So Steve arrived around 4 p.m. and watched it. Then he went off, came back at 10 the next morning, sat down, and played 'Send in the Clowns.' Len and I were standing by the piano, and he played the first half-a-dozen notes, if that, and I had tears in my eyes. I could tell by the timbre of the chords, of those few bars, and I looked at Len and his eyes were full, too."

We also interviewed Cariou about the song.

"'Send in the Clowns' was supposed to be my song. But we changed the dialogue in rehearsal. I was supposed to have a song. Stephen saw the work we had done and the next day came in with 'Send in the Clowns' for Glynis. And he looked at me and said, 'Sorry.'"

How did he feel?

"I was a little pissed off. But what could you say? He sits down and sings 'Send in the Clowns' and your jaw drops. You couldn't say much. But I got to sing the reprise."

Asked if "Now" was a hard song for him to learn, he said:

"Not really. It scans so well. I think having done a lot of classical work and iambic pentameter, it helps a lot when doing Stephen's stuff. There are a lot of inner rhymes, so it wasn't that difficult. But it's the kind of song that goes at a good clip. It was great fun to do [he sings]:"*In view of her penchant/For something romantic,/De Sade is too trenchant/And Dickens too frantic,/And Stendhal would ruin/The plan of attack,/As there isn't much blue in/The Red and the Black.*"

Twenty-five years later, Cariou still remembered the lyrics.

Cariou repeated his role as Fredrik in the film, which has been derided by some. Asked about the film, he said:

"I like the film. I thought it was a rather splendid job. I just don't think it was handled well by the producers. They didn't get a distributor, and had to go begging for one. It should have had a better life, in my opinion, because I think it's lovely."

Patricia Elliott, who played Charlotte, was asked about "Every Day a Little Death." At first, she said, her main song was "My Husband the Pig," but Sondheim said it was "not Charlotte" and wrote the new song for her instead.

"Many people tell me it's their favorite song in the show," she said. "It's a song that touches people in a very deep place. It's written so lightly, but there are these very dark words, so it really accomplished the ironic tone of Charlotte, her self-mocking character. But it's a very difficult song musically. The intervals are really difficult.

"The thing about Stephen's songs is that they are tailor-made for the character, and they can only go one place in the show. And another facet of his huge genius is that he treats you as if you had as much knowledge of the musical theater as he has. He always treated me as if I were a colleague."

Lawrence Guittard talked about "In Praise of Women."

"Originally, Steve wrote kind of military numbers—that was his original idea. Then we got 'Bang' in Boston. And then he wrote a song called 'Women Were Born to Wait.'

"It was a fascinating experience to be part of that. But it was also scary because so much had to be learned so quickly. When you learn to do something quickly, fear is your constant companion."

Guittard said he learned "In Praise of Women" overnight in Boston. He said he and Patricia Elliott, playing Charlotte, were glassy-eyed.

Both stayed through the end of the run in New York, and Guittard played the count again in the movie. He said he never intended to do *Night Music* again, but then came the offer to play Fredrik in the Royal National Theater's *Night Music* in London in 1995.

"Who could resist playing opposite Judi Dench and work at the National Theater?"

The result, he said, was "the best experience in my entire working career, and it restored my belief in working in the theater."

Our *Night Music* anniversary issue also included an analysis of the score by Mark Eden Horowitz, a music specialist at the Library of Congress and a frequent *TSR* contributor. In it, he wrote:

"To my ears, 'You Must Meet My Wife' could be the most beautiful piece of music Sondheim has composed. I've often wished that it had an alternate, more universal lyric, simply so it could be sung more often as a traditional stand-alone love song. Although it can be categorized as a humorous song, the poignancy of the music adds a depth of soul and feeling to Fredrik. Singing of his wife to his ex-mistress is certainly an unusual ploy, but in this case it is appropriate, and inevitably funny, if not also a little sad."

Concluding, he wrote:

"There is a surprising warmth and generosity of spirit in *A Little Night Music*. On the surface, none of its characters is particularly important or significant—their faults are many, even their romances are pitiable. Who cares about these people? Why write a musical about them? It is that very humanity, those universal insecurities as they are expressed in at least some of the songs that command our empathy and sympathy. 'Send in the Clowns' is one of those songs. The song is not ironic even though it is about ironic events; it is confessional, honest and heartfelt. Much of that feeling comes from the music that is both complex and simple. The melody is almost entirely diatonic, save for a series of G naturals in the bridge, and composed of short phrases with few held notes, a trait uncharacteristic of ballads. But the harmonies are deep and troubled, if without the stings of some of the earlier music, and there is a melancholy resignation that becomes painfully beautiful in the bridge."

More LETTERS

S ONDHEIM DID NOT SEND notes about the Spring or Summer issues, but I did receive a letter containing some random comments about the Fall issue, which featured the Carol Burnett *Putting It Together* on the cover.

October 16, 1998

Dear Paul –

The new issue looks good and reads well. A couple of corrections just for the record.

The man with the puffed cheeks in the bottom picture on p. 13 is not Larry Blyden, but Michael Vale.

In the article on Michael Starobin, William Goldman is given credit for Evening Primrose. *As you know, it should be James.*

XXXXX is mistaken when he says that I was working on Do I Hear a Waltz? *when I wrote my version of "Do I Hear a Waltz?" I wrote that two years previously for a television musical called* Do You Hear a Waltz? *(not based on* The Time of the Cuckoo*)—a show that Arthur Laurents and I were going to write but never did.*

Best,

Steve

Our Spring 1999 issue focused on *Anyone Can Whistle*, Sondheim's 1964 flop, with an examination of its score, an excerpt from Angela Lansbury's memoir about the show, and a draft of Sondheim's title song that I found at the Wisconsin Center for Film and Theater Research.

Harvey Evans, who had roles in so many Broadway and regional productions, was one of "Cora's Boys" in the original production and wrote a lengthy piece about the experience. An excerpt:

"In forty-four years of show business, *Anyone Can Whistle* was, and has remained, the most intense theatrical experience I've ever been through. Everything was extreme—the highs, the lows, the passion, the exhilaration, even the intoxication. During the tryout in Philly, we would rush to the Variety Club after every performance to down quite a few scotches and either laugh or cry, depending on how the day went. But even on a bad day, the experience was in no way a negative one. It's just that everything was heightened, probably because of my (and I think the company's) great love and belief in the project."

The issue also included a short Sondheim Q&A:

Q. Meryle Secrest's recent biography is the most extensive look at your personal life you've allowed to date. Why now? And are you satisfied with the book?

A. I knew someone would do an unauthorized biography soon, so I thought it better to beat them to the punch. I thought her biography of Lenny [Bernstein] was the fairest, the least salacious. I'm pleased with how the book turned out.

Our Summer 1999 issue covered the American premiere of *Saturday Night* in Chicago and included another short Sondheim Q&A:

"Q: Is your impulse to write for the musical theater as strong as ever?

"A: Writing is what I do. It's the major thing in my life. So, yes, even when I'm having a bad time at it I still enjoy it."

Meanwhile, the *Wise Guys* saga continued and we seemed to be covering every development—or non-development. Sam Mendes was named director and a three-week workshop was scheduled. Then the workshop was canceled and Weidman said, "Once we got into the performance mode with the pressure to perform, it was difficult to look at the material." A few months later, Hal Prince was suddenly in charge and Sondheim told us: "We hope to do it in a year's time."

Prince had directed several Sondheim shows, from *Company* (1970) to *Merrily We Roll Along* (1981), but they parted ways after *Merrily* flopped.

"To be back in a room with Steve and Hal after having done my first show with them is very exciting," Weidman told us, "and Hal's enthusiasm is infectious."

Sondheim, Weidman, and Prince had worked together on *Pacific Overtures* in 1976.

In March 2000, I attended a service with Dana Ivey (Yvonne/ Naomi Eisen in *Sunday*) at the Unitarian Church of All Souls in New York. The service used portions of Sondheim songs ("Not While I'm Around," "Old Friends," "No One Is Alone," and others) because the hymns and the reading focused on Sondheim's sense of community, and the sermon was entitled "Out of the Woods."

For Forrest Church, minister of All Saints for twenty-two years, it was a natural.

"I've loved Sondheim since *Sweeney Todd*," Church told me. "I've seen everything he's done, including *Assassins*. As a matter of fact, if

I'm going to put an album on for background, it's often *Assassins*. That shows how rabid I am."

Sondheim, Church said, "has the ability to combine the acid with love. He expands our human repertory of understanding. For me personally, there has been no time when Sondheim has not been a personal guide—or a tweak."

After I wrote about the service, Sondheim sent me a note.

March 16, 2000
Dear Paul –
I wish you had let me know about the service—I'd love to have been there. Did anyone by any chance make a recording?
Thanks for the birthday wishes, and for the continued dedication.
As always,
Steve

He also sent me a long fax that took issue with one sentence in the Spring 2000 issue. In an article about a production of *A Little Night Music* in Miskolc, Hungary, the director had criticized "the exorbitant royalties demanded by Music Theater International, which nearly capsized our production with their inflexible, uncooperative approach to the cultural exchange, alas."

In his fax, Sondheim came to MTI's defense, but also attacked the director's "bitter, certainly overstated and possibly inaccurate view of the situation." MTI, he wrote, handled almost all of the shows he'd written, "and I've been their happy client for a very long time. They are the best in the business...MTI has done more to keep musicals alive and thriving than any other organization I can think of."

PHONE CALLS & FAXES

I DIDN'T NOTICE until much later that Sondheim's note about the church service was the last he sent me while I was editor. No more clarifications or "emendations." When I did realize their absence, I wondered 1) if he didn't read *TSR* anymore, 2) if he read it but didn't find anything to write to me about, or 3) if he was now convinced that *The Sondheim Review* was a reputable publication that covered his work thoroughly and impartially and he didn't need to hover over every issue. He was now confident, as he said in his Letter to the Editor, that "the care and authenticity of the articles and reports in the magazine will be used as the basis of future 'scholarship' about the shows."

I hoped it was the last option. I didn't ask and went on with my work.

We continued our long-distance relationship, however, by talking on the phone (thank goodness for tape recorders) and exchanging faxes. This was in the olden days before emails and texting became more common. If Sondheim even used emails, I never got one. I tried to respect his time, but I also wanted news and accurate information for the magazine, so I saved up questions to ask in a single call.

I found that often he was more voluble on the phone, volunteering information about casting, new productions, revisions to scores and scripts. I wish I had saved the tapes.

When a major production of *Merrily We Roll Along* was announced for the Donmar Warehouse in London, I called Sondheim to ask if there would be changes. He said that the director had asked that the opening graduation scene, which had been in the original 1981 production but then cut, be restored "with a difference."

"We'll try it in previews and see if it works," he said.

Apparently it didn't work because it wasn't restored.

A *British* INTERVIEW

A FTER A REVIVAL of *A Little Night Music* opened in London, Sondheim was interviewed on the BBC on various topics:

BBC: Why do you feel the British people have a peculiar love for your work?

SS: I think it's about love of language. The first good reviews I ever got were for the British production of *A Funny Thing Happened on the Way to the Forum*. And I think it has a lot to do with the fact that people over here, probably through—I don't know what, maybe through training in schools, perhaps people going to Shakespeare as opposed to Neil Simon—they listen to language more carefully, I think.

BBC: You've described *A Little Night Music* as being "whipped cream with knives."

SS: Well, yes, it's that, but I think that phrase is from Hal Prince, who directed it originally. The songs that I wrote were too dark for Hal, and so he said he wanted it to be much more "fluffy." And I said then it's going to be lightweight, and he said, "No! No! There can still be knives underneath." It may be a misquote, but the point is I've used that phrase in years subsequent to that discussion. I didn't want it to become frivolous and sentimental. There's a good deal of irony and, to put it immodestly, I always like *Night Music* better than I think I'm going to. And I'm always surprised at how well—and I'm sure I'm evoking the wrath of God here—I'm always surprised at how well it holds up. It's a much stronger piece for something that seems to be more whipped cream than I remembered. I love the phrase "a little night music." I hadn't realized, for example, that "serenade" also means "night music." I hadn't realized how many words mean "night music."

BBC: When you write a piece, how tightly structured is it in your mind [so] that when you get over here and you watch a show, how much of it do you think: They shouldn't do that, I want them to do this!

SS: And now are you talking about a piece that has already been written, or a piece that is first time out?

BBC: When you've written it, how clear in your mind are you about how it should work?

SS: Shows should "look" differently. It's the director's and the designer's vision. This *Night Music* is entirely different compared to the way Hal's production was in 1973. Which is one of the things I like about it. If it looked like Hal's production, then it's not as much fun.

BBC: For whom do you write?

SS: Myself, primarily, but I write for myself as a member of the audience. I want the audience to like or not to like, to understand or be intrigued by something I write, but like most writers, I write something which I would like to stand at the back of the theater and watch, and I think most writers do that.

BBC: What do you think of, for instance, the plays of Andrew Lloyd Webber, which are very popular…Do you regret that your plays are not as popular in terms of…

SS: No, no. I think every writer wants as wide an audience as possible, but you also want to write something you're proud of, and put your name to.

BBC: When you sit and watch a show, what offers you the moment of greatest pleasure?

SS: Oh, what an interesting question! Hmmm, I think it's when I think that I feel a moment is fulfilled, the way I heard and the way I visualized it, and that the audience is getting it. It's very important to me, the communication between the stage and the audience, the way when you tell somebody a story, you want them to get it. If you tell someone a joke, it doesn't matter whether they laugh. Did they get the joke? That's the point, and for me, that's what it's about. It's about an audience understanding what I'm doing and, if they approve, that's just gravy. That's an extra delight. If they understand it and they don't approve, it's disappointing, but it's still in some way fulfilling, so it has to do with intention. If you get your intention across, you're more than halfway home. And then, of course, if at the end of the evening, you feel that they've had a wonderful time, that is the most exhilarating, because that meant they've got it and enjoyed it.

Follies REVIVAL

THE SPRING AND SUMMER 2001 issues covered a revival of _Follies_, the first since the original 1971 production. It would star Blythe Danner as Phyllis, Gregory Harrison as Ben, Treat Williams as Buddy, Judith Ivey as Sally, and Polly Bergen as Carlotta. All were known more for their acting than their singing, and most for work in films rather than theater. It would be directed by Matthew Warchus.

The revival would play at the Roundabout Theater, which had hosted the revival of _Company_ in 1995. It was not the Winter Garden.

I looked forward to this, of course, because I had been so affected by the original production. We asked Sondheim to offer his thoughts about the revival. His response:

"The cast is both good and enthusiastic, and I like the director enormously. Unfortunately, because of budget restrictions, the orchestra will consist of only fourteen musicians, and the scenery and costumes will be nowhere near as elaborate as the 1971 production. But then, the theater is smaller, and the feeling of the show is entirely different.

"We hope that the audience will not come expecting a replica of the original. What it will be is halfway between the surrealism of the original and the realism of the London production, like the Paper Mill version.

"The score will be exactly like that of the original, except that the 'Bolero d'Amour' will probably not be a bolero any more—more likely a foxtrot."

One day after rehearsals on a top floor of Radio City Music Hall, we sat down to interview the show's four principal cast members. As I remember, the room was cold and drafty, and dancers in their leotards kept running through.

TSR: Let's talk about your characters.

Treat Williams: I'm still in the process of getting to know who Buddy is. Each day something new comes about. But basically he's a guy who comes to this party with great trepidation because he's been living with this awareness that his wife has always longed for his ex-best-friend.

So he's concerned about the state of his marriage, whether his wife will rekindle this relationship, and then he has to come to terms with the dilemma he's in, being caught between two women, Margie and Sally. And he realizes the problem lies within him. He's unable to be intimate with anyone, and that's wonderfully expressed in "Buddy's Blues."

Blythe Danner: I think Phyllis is very well drawn in the script. She's someone who was a chorus girl, an innocent girl who came to New York and was a clean piece of paper to be written on. She was very much in love with Ben, and that love was never quite reciprocated, so she learned to exist in this very sophisticated world in order to survive. She became devoid of many of the emotions she would otherwise have had—emotions as a mother, for example, but she was denied that. To survive, she had to create this veneer around herself.

Gregory Harrison: Ben is a very complex character, dysfunctional but charming. Sometimes he's deceptive and doesn't know he is, and sometimes he's deceptive and means to be exactly that. So he's fooling others, he's fooling himself, but at the same time he's not fooling anybody at all. I can't think of characters in any other musical except a Sondheim musical who are such gray characters, not black and white but gray, and who can delineate who they are and support these complex stories by singing these wonderful songs.

Judith Ivey: The biggest clue to Sally for me was in the music. She starts out singing in her belting voice, moves to a mixture of soprano and belt, and then moves to high soprano. And then in "Losing My Mind," she's back in a belt style. For one character to go through all that, well, that was a clue that this woman was not, shall we say, very sedentary. There are obvious clues in the text, but this genius [Sondheim] has a way of depicting a character by musical notes, not just words. So this personifies who she is, someone who is out of control and has many sides.

TSR: How are you approaching the character?

Williams: It's interesting. Buddy's 50, I'm 50. Buddy's married with kids, I'm married with kids. Buddy adores his wife, I adore my wife. All marriages have their ups and downs. I think everyone has relationships in which they don't get everything they want or need. I think that's part of this relationship. Buddy thinks he has the right to go off to this other relationship because he's not dealing with the truth.

Danner: At first, I thought I was not properly cast for this role—I don't know how I'm going to do it. But I feel more secure each day. You know we are given so many things that aren't fully drawn, aren't beautifully fleshed out, so often that's a struggle. But these things are there to be explored.

Harrison: I'm still discovering to some extent, too, but Ben is part of who I am. I do that with every character I've ever played. I find that person in me. I find the attributes that are supposed to be Ben's that do exist within all of us. I have regrets. I've made choices I'm not proud of. I've been in denial about things in my life. I've been involved in betrayals. We've all done that.

Ivey: Just today I've found something—twisting a Kleenex so that the focus is on something very fragile and very manic. I don't know whether or not I'll keep it in, but it's a tool to find the person whose mind is all over the place. If anyone lived in subtext, it would be Sally.

TSR: What are the particular challenges for you?

Williams: Stephen's songs are the biggest challenge. They move the characters forward by light years. There is a lot of self-evaluation in his songs, and there's a kind of working out of your life in the song. It's almost like Shakespearean monologues.

Danner: I know that musically the [original] production was so accomplished, and I'm a bit insecure because I'm not a singer. But to turn this down would be insane. So I don't care. I don't read reviews. I'm just going to plunge in.

Harrison: I've spent years and years learning how to sing the hard way. I haven't studied, and I'm a fool not to have. I haven't done it right, but finally after thirty years of singing in the shower and working my way into musicals, I've discovered the difference between performing a song and acting a song. I feel very comfortable, like I know what I'm doing.

Ivey: I'm terrified of the singing. I pretend that I know how to do it. And then I get myself to voice lessons as often as I can, and I hang on the words of my musical director. I come to this basically clean. This is my first Broadway musical, although I did musicals long ago—truly in my youth. But I'm having the time of my life.

BUT NO REVIVAL could match the original production, and everyone was disappointed in this one. *The New York Times* found it "pale and strangely tentative" and longed for the original:

"The beauty we fell in love with 30 years ago isn't looking so good these days. I ran into her at the Belasco Theater the other night. She's turned all brittle and cynical, and she's thin to the point of emaciation. Worst of all, she seems to have lost any real sense of who she is. Sad, isn't it, what the years can do to a great musical?"

The *New York Post* criticized Warchus' "drab and unimaginative staging...which has little idea of the style needed."

On the other hand, the *New York Daily News* applauded Warchus' approach: "The current revival does best with an area that often suffers—telling the basic story of the two former chorus girls, Phyllis and Sally, and their then-beaus, now husbands, Ben and Buddy. By casting good actors in these roles, director Matthew Warchus has rein-forced the spine of the show. They can make scenes convincing that often seem forced."

In *Newsday*, Linda Winer became vehement about the casting:

"So what," she wrote, "if the exquisite Danner, as society-wife Phyllis, can barely sing and looks trapped in headlights when required to dance? Who cares if the feisty Ivey, as Sally from Phoenix, sings with all the abandon of a conscientious student and has been sentenced

SONDHEIM & Me

to fight for love in a matronly dress? But care, we do. In this city of unemployed musical talent, it is incomprehensible that such a massively desirable, highly scrutinized, wildly adored, and historically significant project is not bursting with one breakout performance after another."

For myself, after being so enthralled with the original production, this revival was more realistic, even gritty. I liked some of the supporting cast: It was thrilling to see Joan Roberts, the original Laurie in *Oklahoma!*, as Heidi Schiller, Marge Champion, from those old MGM movies, as Emily Whitman, and Betty Garrett as Hattie Walker. But a musical shouldn't be remembered by three minutes-long performances.

Follies closed after 117 performances.

Assassins DELAYED

T HE FALL 2001 ISSUE announced that *Assassins*, which had run at that tiny theater off-Broadway in 1990-91, would have a Broadway production opening on November 29, 2001. Neil Patrick Harris would be both the Balladeer and Lee Harvey Oswald. I asked Sondheim if the political climate had changed since the Gulf War ten years earlier, a reason sometimes given for the show's failure to move to Broadway.

"I don't think the so-called political climate has much effect on audience perception," he said. "When we opened [off-Broadway] ten years ago, some thought the coincidence of the Gulf War affected public perception of the show. I'm reluctant to assign the blame to such things, but I suppose that some thought we weren't patriotic enough. The show isn't about the presidents, though—it's about these individuals and their specific reasons for doing what they did."

His statement turned out to be premature. On September 11, 2001, militant Islamic terrorists attacked the country, and the Winter 2002 issue reported that *Assassins* was postponed. Sondheim and John Weidman issued a statement acknowledging that a show about killing presidents would be difficult for audiences at that time.

"*Assassins* is a show which asks audiences to think critically about various aspects of the American experience," they said. "In light of Tuesday's murderous assault on our nation and on the most fundamental things in which we all believe, we, the Roundabout, and director Joe Mantello believe this is not an appropriate time to present a show which makes such a demand."

When I asked Sondheim about this, he said: "We were afraid that audiences wouldn't understand what we were saying so soon after the events in September. It wasn't fear of being accused of being unpatriotic again—it was just that audiences wouldn't be able to understand."

Then the troubled show about the Mizner brothers, whose title had changed from W*ise Guys* to *Gold!,* became involved in a legal battle. Sondheim and Weidman said they owned the rights to the property. The theater producer Scott Rudin said he did. The issue went to the courts but was resolved by the time we published another issue.

ON MOTIFS, PASTICHE, AND BEING AN *Icon*

O**N MARCH 26 2001**, just five days after his 71st birthday, a relaxed and affable Stephen Sondheim took the stage at the sold-out Walter Reade Theater at Lincoln Center. The evening was part of *The New York Times* Speaker Series and associate editor Sean Patrick Flahaven was there to record excerpts from Sondheim's comments.

ON THE JAPANESE PRODUCTION OF *PACIFIC OVERTURES*, WHICH WOULD BE PART OF THE KENNEDY CENTER'S SONDHEIM CELEBRATION NEXT YEAR:

"It's one of the best things I've ever seen, and I urge you all to see it. The director, Amon Miyamoto, is something of a genius."

ON STUDYING WITH MILTON BABBITT:

"We studied thematic development and analysis. He taught me what he called the 'archetectonics' of a piece, where motifs dictate the larger structure. It's also called 'long-line composition.' Music exists in time, so how do you organize it in time? The concept is of enormous help to plot out a song. We analyzed Kern's 'All the Things You Are,' which is built on a harmonic structure unlike any other song."

ON THE USE OF RECURRING RHYTHMIC, MELODIC, AND HARMONIC MOTIFS:

"I think it's valuable to the mostly musically uneducated listeners because it's still felt, even if you don't know the technicalities. James Lapine does it with words. If you read the script of *Sunday in the Park with George* closely, you'll realize that he repeats words and phrases throughout."

ON THE PASTICHE SONGS IN FOLLIES:

"I was imitating the first-rate composers I love: Kern, Gershwin, Arlen, Porter—I love to delve into their music to see what makes their songs sound unique. My goal was to imitate their styles, not to write for period characters. 'Losing My Mind' is based on Gershwin's 'The Man I Love.' It's affectionate—I'm never making fun of them. I was only a smart-ass once: 'Please Hello' in *Pacific Overtures*. I don't like Gilbert and Sullivan, so I decided to imitate their style but rhyme three times as much as they did."

ON THE BURDEN OF BEING A LIVING ICON:

"You've hit a nerve. I don't know how to deal with [audience expectations]. It's very difficult, and it's one of the reasons I'm slowing down. *Wise Guys* has been in the works for five years, and the show is *this* big [holds hands a foot apart], not a huge show [extends arms fully]. I'm afraid people are going to say, 'It took five years for that?!'" [Laughter]

ON NOT WRITING OPENLY GAY CHARACTERS, YET APPEALING TO GAY AUDIENCES:

"Are there openly gay characters in Shakespeare? The fact that you have to think about it means probably not. Larry Kramer once suggested that I write a show about gay issues. But I don't write about topics—I'm only interested in writing stories. I also don't deliberately write about ethnic minorities, which is not to say that if I found a story I liked about ethnic minorities, I wouldn't jump at it."

ON ANYONE CAN WHISTLE:

"The Kennedy Center was considering it as part of their series, so I talked to Arthur [Laurents] about revising the first twenty minutes or so, which are the biggest problem. But I think it may be insoluble. Its objects of satire are out of date—it's a period piece that's now very dated."

ON THE SOURCE OF THE CHARACTER OF PRODUCER JOE JOSEPHSON IN *MERRILY WE ROLL ALONG:*

"The inspiration for that came from auditioning the *Forum* score before George Abbott. Leonard Bernstein and I had auditioned *West Side Story* for him to produce years before. After I played through part of *Forum*, he said, 'At least it doesn't have any more of that Prokofiev stuff!'"

THE KENNEDY CENTER
Celebration

THE ISSUES of 2002 were dominated by coverage of the Sondheim Celebration at the Kennedy Center in Washington. The four-month $10 million celebration began on May 10 with *Sweeney Todd* and continued in repertory on following weekends with *Company, Sunday in the Park with George, Merrily We Roll Along, Passion*, and *A Little Night Music*. The Tokyo production of *Pacific Overtures* was presented separately.

Stars included Brian Stokes Mitchell, Christine Baransky, Raul Esparza, Rebecca Luker, Judy Kuhn, John Barrowman, Michael Hayden, Melissa Errico, and Lynn Redgrave. Directors were Erik D. Schaeffer, Sean Mathias, Mark Brokaw, and Christopher Ashley.

The Library of Congress sponsored a series of talks in conjunction with the shows.

This was clearly the Sondheim event of the decade if not the century. I went to all of the shows and wrote a lot of stories.

Mark Eden Horowitz, the Library of Congress archivist, reviewed all of the productions for *The Sondheim Review*. Here are excerpts:

Sweeney Todd: "*Sweeney Todd* was an auspicious start to the Kennedy Center Celebration—a strong production of the most demanding of the shows. There was no radical rethinking, and the look and feel owed much to the original 1979 production.

"But there were differences. This was a funnier and sexier production. With Brian Stokes Mitchell as Sweeney, it made sense that Lucy would have loved him foolishly, that Mrs. Lovett would have saved his razors just in case he might return, that he would have the revenge-driven determination and physical strength to escape from Botany Bay, and that Mrs. Lovett would use her wiles to seduce and keep him. And Christine Baranski's Mrs. Lovett had more wiles than most."

Company: "The *Company* at the Kennedy Center is a funny show—a very funny show. The scenes play like great review sketches: a combination of one-liners and character comedy. In fact, this is the first *Company* I've seen in which the scenes worked better than the songs—in most cases. Ultimately, this was a *Company* that was less than the sum of its parts. Probably, because this Bobby [played by John Barrowman] never really became ready for—or worthy of—a partner."

Sunday in the Park with George: "Raul Esparza as George, and Melissa Errico as Dot, both gave extraordinarily rich and nuanced performances. They took some time to warm to. At first, Dot seemed too elegant and refined, and George too prissy and spoiled. But the relationship between them seemed so real that their scenes together were, at times, embarrassingly intimate for the most voyeuristic of audiences. Errico is stunningly beautiful, and has a creamy soprano with a metallic edge and easy pitch. Esparza doesn't have as exciting an instrument as Mandy Patinkin, but it's strong and rich, more real, less ethereal."

Merrily We Roll Along: "The irony of this production of *Merrily We Roll Along* was that its strengths more clearly revealed the show's weaknesses. This *Merrily* was an audience-pleaser—fast, funny, show-bizzy—a real musical comedy. The audience clearly understood that the show ran backward. But as the most uninteresting character in the show, Franklin Shepard seemed unworthy of the musical that surrounded him. The bigger surprise was that it now seems less clear what mistakes or wrong choices are being made and by whom."

Passion: "It may be that this *Passion* will prove to be the most significant of the Kennedy Center productions. The director, Eric Schaeffer, had previously directed an excellent *Passion* at his Signature Theater—perhaps his best effort there. And while this production shared many similarities in design and feel with that one, it was clear that Schaeffer's connection with and understanding of the work have deepened, and he has solved many of the problems with the show."

A Little Night Music: "The summer night smiled broadly on the Kennedy Center's production of *A Little Night Music*, the sixth and last of its Sondheim Celebration. It managed to perfectly balance the disparate elements: the drawing-room farce versus the darker undercurrents, the funny versus the moving, the romantic versus the sexy, the sophisticated versus the earthy. The casting of Blair Brown as Desiree may have raised eyebrows, but she turned out to be wonderful."

The Japanese production of *Pacific Overtures* by the New National Theater, first seen in Tokyo in 2000, was imported to the Kennedy Center to conclude the Sondheim Celebration. The book and lyrics were translated into Japanese, with most of the original English lyrics and text projected onto a large screen in supertitles.

Reviewing the show, Eric Grode, an assistant editor of *TSR*, wrote: "Most of us experience poems visually, so it somehow seemed appropriate that 'There Is No Other Way' and 'Poems' were read as they were heard. Every once in a while, though, the barrage of language was overpowering. The intertwining come-ons of 'Pretty Lady' grew a bit monotonous as one undifferentiated set of lines, and the translator appeared to have given up with 'Please Hello'—only about one-third of the lyrics were even displayed."

SONDHEIM ON THE Celebration

A FTER THE CELEBRATION concluded, the Review's Sean Patrick Flahaven sat down with Sondheim at his Manhattan home to reflect on the festival.

TSR: What was your reaction when the celebration was first proposed?

SS: Flattered and embarrassed, in equal amounts.

TSR: What was your involvement in casting?

SS: I decided to let each director have his own way. I asked them to run their selections by me, in case there was anybody I would think would be miscast or wrong for the role, which rarely happened. The first time I saw the actors and gave notes was at each show's run-through in Washington, and then a week later, I went down for two dress rehearsals, two previews, and sometimes the opening performance. Otherwise, the only meetings I had were a dinner with the four directors here in New York, and of course meetings with Eric Schaeffer [the artistic director of the celebration] and Michael Kaiser [president of the Kennedy Center].

TSR: You've stated in a previous interview that you encouraged the directors to find their own interpretations. Yet the six productions were not radically different from the originals.

SS: That's true. Those were their choices, and the restrictions of the material: You can't do S*unday in the Park* about a guy who cuts off his ear. The shows that lend themselves most to "reinterpretation" are *Company, Merrily*, and *Passion*. But *Sweeney?* In a proscenium arch, there isn't a lot you can do differently. In *Sunday*, Eric did extraordinary things visually. I suppose it does lend itself to new interpretation in that way.

TSR: Did any of the directors propose unusual ideas that you thought wouldn't work?

SS: No, nothing startling. Of the six shows, the most abstract and open to interpretation is the opening to *Merrily*. Everything else is more conservative.

TSR: Did you see the designers' plans in advance?

SS: I did, but because I have an ordinary eye, it all looked swell to me. I couldn't fully imagine what it would look like. I just trusted Derek McLane [the set designer]—I knew his work from *Saturday Night*, which was terrific—and it seemed that he and Howell Binkley [the lighting designer] knew what they wanted.

TSR: Given the short rehearsal period and repertory performance schedule, was the production process somewhat like high-pressure summer stock?

SS: No, it's not summer stock, because most of the performers would not operate under the old two-week summer stock rehearsal period. This is a professional, four-and-a-half week rehearsal process. What is restricted is the tech rehearsal period.

When I grew up in the theater, tech rehearsal was two to four days. In the '60s and '70s, suddenly that period started to stretch. Today, tech often takes up to three weeks for a Broadway musical. That's just for adding sets, lighting, costumes, and sound. In Washington, Derek and Howell worked on all six shows with their respective costume designers, and were able to tech each show in three-and-a-half days. And every single show is teched virtually perfectly. If that process could be done on Broadway that way, it would save an enormous amount of money.

I think that the various unions charge more in New York because it's commercial theater. In Washington, however, the stage managers and crew loved what they were doing and made a point of telling me so. Considering that they were working on some weekends to change sets for three shows in repertory, I don't know what the overtime was. All I know is that the shows were budgeted so that they had to be teched in three-and-a-half days, and they did it. Every show, whatever one might think of it, looks professional. That's not just dedication, either—that's skill.

TSR: Having seen so many productions of your work over the years, what was your reaction to seeing them presented all together?
SS: I was impressed by the variety.

TSR: Was there any disadvantage to seeing them all together?
SS: None.

TSR: Were there any standout moments?

SS: Yeah—the audience reactions.

TSR: How did that compare to the audience reactions to the original productions?

SS: Oh, much better, and more energetic.

TSR: Was it a special treat to hear the full orchestrations?

SS: Obviously, it was terrific to hear a big orchestra play *Company, Sweeney Todd,* and *A Little Night Music.* For *Merrily,* we had to use the smaller orchestration because of the changes in the score that Jonathan [Tunick] hadn't fully orchestrated, and the Kennedy Center understandably couldn't afford to commission new orchestrations.

I'll tell you one thing: I've never known a conductor of a musical to get a standing ovation. It only happened one night, at the beginning of the second act of *Company,* when the conductor usually gets a hand. Suddenly, Jonathan got a standing ovation. I know that part of the reason was that the audience knew his whole career, and there he was, conducting one of his most spectacular orchestrations.

TSR: In watching each production, are there moments you still wish you could revise?

SS: Oh, sure. In any show, yes, there's something you wish you could solve.

TSR: Any examples?

SS: In *Sweeney Todd,* I wanted very much to make the scene in which Mrs. Lovett sings "Wait" into a musical scene. It seemed to me too much like a song in the middle of the scene. And the same thing is true in the scene with Mrs. Lovett and the Beadle in the second act. I'd like to go back to Chris Bond's adaptation and write a trio in which Mrs. Lovett is trying to poison the Beadle and the glasses get switched. So at the same time that she's cajoling him into singing the parlor songs, she's getting the drinks and poisoning them. Then Tobias would join in from the cellar in a comic trio. That's the kind of thing I sometimes think about when I look at these shows. But revising old work isn't easy—getting yourself into an "old mode."

TSR: Does seeing the shows in the celebration inspire new creativity?

SS: Just the reverse.

TSR: When you were interviewed for the CBS Sunday Morning piece on the celebration, you were asked what you would say to Oscar Hammerstein if he could have seen the shows, and you responded, "Aren't you proud of me?" What else would you say?

SS: That's pretty much it. He died in 1960, which was before *Forum*, which he would have loved, because he had a bawdy sense of humor. He would have been intrigued and probably disapproved of *Anyone Can Whistle*. But he probably would have approved of the effort at doing something weird, like *Allegro*. It's like what Cameron Mackintosh said to me: "I've been spending my life trying to fix *Allegro*."

TSR: Did you have any hope for the productions transferring to New York?

SS: No, that wasn't in anybody's mind. First of all, we cast people who wouldn't have been available for a long run. The whole idea was to do them in Washington, and that's it. There was never any intention of moving them.

INTO THE WOODS Revival

T HE WINTER 2002 issue announced that a revival of *Into the Woods* starring Vanessa Williams as The Witch and John McMartin as The Narrator would have a tryout in Los Angeles before opening in New York on April 30, 2002.

I called Sondheim to see if there would be changes.

"We might include 'Our Little World' from the London production," he said. "And we might fiddle with the ending, but that wouldn't really involve changing the score."

He said he and book writer James Lapine wanted to experiment in rehearsal with restoring material cut from the San Diego tryout of the original *Woods* in 1986.

"We might restore a seven-minute number called 'Second Midnight' that was reduced to a fragment in the original production."

"Our Little World" was added in the revival. "Second Midnight" was not.

Remembering the original *Woods*, we interviewed Bernadette Peters (BP).

TSR: James Lapine has said he was surprised when you actually volunteered to play The Witch when they were looking for someone after the San Diego tryout. Why did you volunteer?

BP: Because there was something about it, and they needed a Witch. I had learned so much about life in *Sunday*, and I thought that here was another chance, another experience that moves me along in life.

TSR: Did the role change when you took over?

BP: Basically it was there. They had workshopped it, and I knew it was about the show, not me. I didn't want something like "I'm in the show now." I was there to be a part of it, to support the show.

TSR: Some have said that The Witch isn't really integrated into the show. How would you answer that?

BP: James thought of her as not being like other people. She was the only one who would tell them the truth. She was the outsider. She would tell Rapunzel that we're not like other people. And she read them the riot act in "Last Midnight." That's what she was supposed to be.

TSR: What was the most moving moment in the show for you?

BP: So many. I loved listening to it under the stage. "No One Is Alone." Chip Zien singing "No More." "Giants in the Sky." I loved "Children Will Listen" at the end. That's what I waited for.

TSR: *Into the Woods* is one of Sondheim's most performed shows. What is it about it that makes it so popular?

BP: I think it's because it's family oriented. Everyone can enjoy it— fathers, mothers, kids.

TSR: What do you think of reviving it now?

BP: It's a good idea because you'll be getting fathers and mothers and their kids all going to the theater.

TSR: What would you say if they asked you to be The Witch again?

BP: They're getting a whole new cast, so I don't have to think about it.

In his *Sondheim Review* analysis of the score, Steve Swayne, an assistant professor of music at Dartmouth College, wrote:

"It is not often that a musical gets revived less than fifteen years after it left Broadway. Such is the strength of *Into the Woods*, which has reached farther faster and touched audiences more deeply than any of the other shows for which Stephen Sondheim wrote both music and lyrics. Its message, its words, and its tunes strike an elemental chord in us all. *Into the Woods*, like the characters that populate its pages, has had an almost storybook existence.

"Just as the tales it tells weave spells on those who listen, so too does the music manage to enchant and haunt because of its simplicity. Just think of some of the lyrics and the tunes that carry them along. 'Into the Woods' skips along as a schoolgirl might. 'Giants in the Sky' sounds as though someone has found the perfect echo chamber. And 'No One Is Alone' soothes and lulls and comforts and consoles.

"This simplicity, of course, did not come to Sondheim by accident. It is a controlled simplicity, the work of a master craftsman who disguised his exertion in order to make the finished product look (and sound) effortless. And as with many well-crafted pieces, it is in the attention to patterns and repetitions that both the effortlessness and the craft present themselves.

"To better understand this crafted effortlessness, consider what Sondheim has said about the score, quoted in Stephen Banfield's *Sondheim's Broadway Musicals*:

"'There are certain themes in *Woods* that come out of nowhere and go nowhere—songs or song ideas that are never finished. In this respect, *Woods* is closest to *Merrily We Roll Along*, in that I decided to use musical ideas not as developmental leitmotifs, but in the functional way you would use modular furniture. The same theme becomes an inner voice, an accompaniment, a counterpoint. It may be fragmented, but it is not really developed.'"

The *Into the Woods* revival opened on April 30, 2002, at the Broadhurst Theater. In our review, assistant editor Eric Grode wrote:

"Even with a tap-dancing cow and a maypole dance and a slinky witch, the new Broadway revival of *Into the Woods* is hardly a romp through the forest. This may be one of the more faithful revivals in recent memory, but Stephen Sondheim and James Lapine have still found a few dark—and impressive—new wrinkles to their amalgamation of fairy tales as filtered through Freud, Jung, and especially Bettelheim.

"Much has been made of this production's more audience-friendly innovations. Yes, Jack's beloved cow Milky-White, formerly a portable hunk of scenery, is now a talented (if occasionally overindulgent) actor in a cow suit, complete with sad eyes and exposed ribs. And yes, choreographer John Carrafa has introduced a bit more dancing.

"Purists may have problems with Vanessa Williams as The Witch. With the exception of Madonna in *Dick Tracy*, I'm hard-pressed to think of another pop icon injecting a Sondheim role with so many pop mannerisms, and even that comparison falls short.

"Williams, so impressive a few years back replacing Chita Rivera in *Kiss of the Spider Woman*, never quite displays the force to impose herself as the fulcrum of all the various plot machinations. Even with the inclusion of 'Our Little World,' The Witch still feels like an outsider dramaturgically as well as narratively."

Here is a sampling of the critics' views on the revival of *Into the Woods*:

The New York Times: "A bright and beckoning path cuts through the fairy-tale thicket of whimsy and woe that is *Into the Woods*, the musical by Stephen Sondheim and James Lapine that opened last night in a new revival at the Broadhurst Theater. This path is no trail of bread crumbs.

"It is Mr. Sondheim's score, which now shows every sign of enduring into happily-ever-after posterity, that keeps leading you onward in a show that does not inspire confidence on all levels. Trust in Mr. Sondheim, though. Follow the music. It will take you somewhere wonderful.

"It should probably come as no surprise that *Into the Woods*, first staged on Broadway only fifteen years ago, remains as mixed a blessing as the fulfilled wishes of the show's ever-dissatisfied characters. Mr. Sondheim has written songs that are indeed like fairy tales in their simplicity and echoing depths."

New York Daily News: "The show has always had its awkward moments, but the original cast was so perfect you could easily overlook them. With a few exceptions, that cannot be said of the current group, which is, for the most part, charmless....The original *Into the*

Woods reflected a desire to dig into these ancient stories to find their meaning. The revival seems merely a bid for the lucrative family market on post-Disney Broadway."

Variety: "With some splashy special effects, fleet choreography by John Carrafa, and performers who bring piles of sass, wit, and sparkle to their roles, this is a flashier and blessedly brisker presentation of Sondheim and Lapine's crazy quilt of fairy tales for our unhappy-ever-after age. No, it doesn't solve the problems of a show that still lacks cohesion and concision—and, on a deeper level, authentic emotional appeal. But in taking itself less seriously, the new production does render those flaws less deleterious, and it allows the gems in Sondheim's score to glitter bewitchingly."

Into the Woods won the 2002 Tony award for best revival and ran for 299 performances.

SWEENEY TODD AS *Opera*

MOVING FROM the musical stage, where it usually plays, to the opera house, *Sweeney Todd* was given a spectacular production by the Lyric Opera of Chicago in November 2002. *TSR* covered it in our Winter 2003 issue.

Opera superstar Bryn Terfel was Sweeney and, our critic said "the sheer volume and resonance of his bass-baritone enabled him to communicate the enormity of Sweeney's rage." His vocal presence, according to the critic, enabled him to create a Sweeney large enough to touch all in a 3,563-seat opera house.

The world-caliber cast included Judith Christin as Mrs. Lovett, Nathan Gunn as Anthony, Celena Shafer as Johanna, and Timothy Nolen as Judge Turpin. There was a thirty-member chorus and a seventy-six piece orchestra conducted by Sondheim's primary music director, Paul Gemignani.

In a program a few days before the opening, Sondheim was asked about the ominous music played when Sweeney slits the throats of his customers.

"I made two resolutions," Sondheim said. "The first is that when you expect someone to be murdered, he isn't. And the second moment is that when you don't expect it, he is."

The first, he said, was when Sweeney was interrupted as he was about to cut Judge Turpin's throat. The second was when he sings a "sweet tune" while murdering one after another of his innocent customers. "It's such a shocker."

Sondheim said he wrote the "Lullaby" for the Beggar Woman's scene at the end because too many people did not know that she was Sweeney's wife. Knowing that makes her murder terrifying.

In answer to other questions, Sondheim said:

• After seeing the production of *Company* at the Kennedy Center Sondheim Celebration, he was able to articulate something about the show that he had never done before. What *Company* is really about, he said, is growing up, about responsibility, about becoming responsible for your own life.

• Over the last five or ten years, he hasn't written with the constant intensity he had earlier in his career. Perhaps it is age, he admitted. He is a firm believer in creativity being done in dreams, but that only happens when "you saturate yourself," and he's "doing exactly that with *Gold!*"

• Working as a lyricist with Leonard Bernstein, Jule Styne, and Richard Rodgers was each a different experience. "Lenny liked to work in collaboration in a room together. We worked one day together and two days apart. I'm a slow writer, and it's hard for me to be in a room with a collaborator. Styne was enormously facile—maybe the word is fertile. I wrote a section of the lyrics first and then outlined the rest where the music should rise or fall. For Rodgers, I outlined the rises and falls, but when it came to the ballads, he wrote the tunes first."

• "Everything I've written is supposedly autobiographical," Sondheim said, "whether it's Bobby in *Company* or Seurat in *Sunday in the Park with George.*"

He said people identify him with Seurat and see his song "Finishing the Hat" as especially personal.

"It's about someone who makes something out of nothing, which is what an artist does, and that's what the song is about. In one sense, it's about every artist in the world, and I am one, so, of course, it's about me, too. Most people think art is talent. I wanted to make it look like hard work. All those dots on that canvas, and there are some 100,000 dots—they're really blobs—each one is a choice, and all those choices combine to make that work of art happen. Art is hard work. It takes just as much hard work to make a bad painting as it does to make a good one. It is always flattering when someone says, 'Oh, you're so talented.' But what I want to tell them is, 'Yes, I'm talented, but I work hard. I don't sit down and out comes [he sings here] 'Some enchanted evening...'

"Richard Rodgers was famous for writing tunes like that, but what you don't know is that he thought about it for days. Oscar [Hammerstein] would hand him a lyric and he would marinate it. He just didn't sit down and do it. But when he did go to the piano, because he was facile, he was able to do it. Jule Styne was the same way."

THE YOUNG ONES IN *Concert*

ONE OF THE MOST ENJOYABLE Sondheim evenings I ever had was in January 2003 in Ann Arbor, Michigan. The four "young ones" in the original production of *Follies* came on stage and assumed the roles of the "adult" performers in the show. Thus, Kurt Peterson became Ben (John McMartin), Harvey Evans was Buddy (Gene Nelson), Virginia Sandifur was Phyllis (Alexis Smith), and Marti Rolph was Sally (Dorothy Collins). They were joined by Donna McKechnie playing the role of Carlotta (Yvonne De Carlo).

Thirty-three years after the original, they made no attempt to imitate their predecessors. Even with the truncated script used in the concert, they found their own interpretations of the characters and the songs.

On the Sunday morning after the concert, they gathered to talk to *TSR* about the event. Here are some excerpts from the piece we published in the Spring 2003 issue:

TSR: **Can you talk about how the show was put together?**

Evans: Remember how we had to be there every time the big people were there, and it got tiresome. Because it kept changing constantly, rotating, adding on to, and you never knew how important you were because it hadn't been put together.

Rolph: And our parts, well, really the whole show, was very fragmented. You would run in and say four lines and disappear. I didn't have any sense of the whole show.

Evans: We didn't see it come together until late in the process. I read the script and I said, "Ohhhh, what is this?"

Sandifur: Remember we went through this whole process of wondering when we were a ghost and when we were our present selves. Hal [Prince] was working on that film technique, and we couldn't remember when we were supposed to come on with the white ghost makeup or when we had the regular makeup. We must have had nine layers of makeup.

Evans: And no skin left.

TSR: **A lot of people didn't like it.**

Rolph: People were polarized. Some people loved it and came fifty times. Some hated it. There was no middle ground.

Evans: It was the year of *No, No, Nanette*, the year of nostalgia.

Rolph: The title was *Follies* and I think people not involved in the theater were expecting a Follies kind of show.

Sandifur: The Rockettes.

Evans: Also, Hal did some staging that was pretty avant-garde, very filmatic. One couple would be in a room on one side of the stage, and another couple would be in a room on the other side, and there was cross-cutting. We weren't used to Pinter then.

Sandifur: Somebody said it's supposed to be a musical *Virginia Woolf.* I guess people weren't ready for it.

TSR: Can you talk about the "Who's That Woman" number?

Rolph: What happened was the stage was raked. It was actually on three different angles. It was very hard to dance with tap shoes and you could slip. There were a lot of injuries. And those mirror costumes were about twenty-five pounds apiece.

Sandifur: They had real mirrors and they were cut so that every time the tutus went up, they would slice our arms and we'd say, "We're bleeeeeeding!"

Rolph: It's hard to dance when you're bleeding.

Sandifur: They covered them with plastic, and then they gave us gloves.

Rolph: So in the middle of rehearsals, they decided they had to take the taps off some of the shoes because it was too dangerous, but they needed the tap sound, so they had Steve Boockvor, Mary Jane Houdina, Roy Barry—all these dancers—in the basement with microphones. And there was also additional tape of the singing because everyone was out of breath on stage. So they had singing and dancing coming from the basement.

TSR: What was Hal Prince doing?

Sandifur: Hal made sure that everyone was on the same page.

Peterson: Like telling Steve to go home and write!

Evans: And he also said, "That's not a good-enough ending. Let's have a better ending."

Sandifur: He would say the ending wasn't correct, and you'd see James [Goldman] go off into a corner and take out his pen and you could see by his body language who he was writing for. He would get into the character, and then he would start writing.

TSR: **And Sondheim during all this?**

Peterson: He was hands on. He would come and put his arm around you and say, "Now, on this word here, 'If you think you LOVED today.'" And he spoke to us on a level that I wasn't intimidated by him. I'd be more intimidated now than I was at 22.

Rolph: He chooses every word so carefully. You hear something as a throwaway, and then when you really get into the script, you think, "Oh, my gosh. He chose 'I should have worn green' instead of 'I meant to wear green.'"

Peterson: I wouldn't trade being in the original *Follies* for anything. It was the most important show in my career, and then I had the association with Steve and the people I would never have met. It changed my life. It changed my life.

Gypsy REVIVED

THE SUMMER 2003 issue reported on the revival of *Gypsy* that starred Bernadette Peters and was directed by Sam Mendes. It had been revived twice after the original Ethel Merman production in 1959, the first starring Angela Lansbury in 1974 and the second with Tyne Daly in 1989.

After the opening on May 1, 2003, Eric Grode, our associate editor, reviewed the show for *TSR*:

"As you've likely heard (or simply knew all along), Bernadette Peters is no Ethel Merman. She's no Angela Lansbury and no Tyne Daly, either. But she is Bernadette Peters, and the qualities that have served her so well in the past—her winsome charm and porcelain beauty—take on surprising resonances in the highly entertaining revival of *Gypsy*.

"That Peters' gutsy, wounded take on Mama Rose never—well, almost never—disrupts the piece's incredible balance is a testament to Sam Mendes. His direction may occasionally veer toward the frantic, but he and Peters provide a sturdy framework for a complicated and very rewarding approach on the life of Gypsy Rose Lee. Forty-four years and three previous Broadway productions haven't dimmed the sharp edges of Jule Styne, Stephen Sondheim, and Arthur Laurents' dazzling, harrowing masterpiece one bit.

"Peters has little of the white-knuckle ferocity that Merman and Daly brought to the part. Tessie Tura points out that Rose could have stripped in her day, but Peters' Rose is equally plausible as a former child star. This is a Rose who's still 'got it'—and who knows it. A Rose who plausibly got close to the brass ring herself, close enough to spend a lifetime lunging for it vicariously. A Rose who had little trouble snagging three husbands and almost understands why each one left.

"Any *Gypsy* will inevitably be measured by its Mama Rose. And ready or not, folks, here comes an extremely pleasant surprise. What with the misbegotten *Annie Get Your Gun* revival, a subpar *Goodbye Girl*, and various half-baked TV and film projects, it's been more than fifteen years since Bernadette Peters has had a vehicle worthy of her talents. Hold your hats and hallelujah. Bernadette is gonna show it to you."

Other critics:

The New York Times: "You can tear down the black crepe, boys. Take the hearse back to the garage, and start popping Champagne corks. Mama's pulled it off, after all—big time.

"Playing a role that few people thought would ever fit her and shadowed by vultures predicting disaster, Bernadette Peters delivered the surprise coup of many a Broadway season in the revival of *Gypsy* that opened last night at the Shubert Theater.

"Ms. Peters, a beloved eternal daughter of the American musical, has taken on that genre's most daunting maternal role: Mama Rose, the ultimate stage mother in the ultimate backstage show and a part cast in bronze by Ethel Merman more than four decades ago. Working against type and expectation under the direction of Sam Mendes, Ms. Peters has created the most complex and compelling portrait of her long career, and she has done this in ways that deviate radically from the Merman blueprint."

New York Daily News: "Peters still is too much a kewpie doll to be plausible as the stage mother who, in her sick drive for success, makes her daughter a stripper....Her Mama Rose is charming, which is accurate if you read June Havoc's splendid memoir, *Early Havoc.* The Rose that Laurents wrote, however, is darker, and Peters seldom conveys her ruthlessness."

Newsday: "Mendes' production is by no means a disaster. It is merely a conventional, ordinary, stolidly professional and routine retelling of one of the last and one of the most important of the golden-age American musical comedies, a time when story, music, dance, and spectacle co-existed in some magical balance.....Peters' Mama Rose is suitably indomitable, but oddly uninteresting."

The show ran for a respectable 451 performances.

TRANSLATIONS

O NE OF MY FAVORITE parts of editing *The Sondheim Review* was reading about Sondheim productions in other countries and how his clever and precise lyrics had been translated. I think we published at least one story about an international production in every issue.

From *Company* in an amphitheater in Athens to *Putting It Together* in a suburb of Cape Town to *Into the Woods* in Shanghai to *Passion* in Manila, Sondheim shows were being presented all around the world. And that meant his lyrics had to be translated for local audiences.

Obviously, this is a daunting challenge. How, for example, do you translate funny lines like *"Popping pussies into pies"* or *"I telephoned my analyst about it and he said to see him Monday, but by Monday I'll be floating in the Hudson with the other garbage"* into Italian or Japanese?

With some difficulty, but translators all over the world were doing it then (and still are).

This brings to mind the story we published in the Fall 2003 issue about the adventurous Bernstein School of Musical Theater in Bologna presenting *Sweeney Todd* (this in the land of Verdi and Puccini). The job of translating was given to Andrea Ascari, a graduate of the school.

"First," he told us, "I sang and played the songs for months, just to enter the peculiar musical world of *Sweeney* and to have all the melodies and syllables (and rhymes!) in my throat.

"Then I had to face the harsh reality: Italian has a more complex syntactic structure than English, with longer words and a limited use of onomatopoeia. How could I render verses like 'fishies splashing' or 'seagull squawking'?

"While working, I felt a deep connection with the verses, the style, the characters, the 'fearful symmetries' of the score. When I felt friction or frustration—or murderous intents—I practiced meditation or went to sleep (what nightmares!), confident that a natural solution would come the next day.

"I worked from November to June, and I have to admit that I'm really proud of the achievement. I had feared that the Italian public couldn't have fun with the black humor of the play, which is so distant from our Mediterranean taste. I'm happy to say that I was totally wrong. The show was a big success and a step forward in the introduction of Sondheim in Italy."

An example:

I feel you,
Johanna,
I feel you.
I was half convinced I'd waken,
Satisfied enough to dream you.
Happily I was mistaken,
Johanna!

Ti sento, Johanna,
Ti sento.
Io pensavo di svegliarmi,

Soddisfatto di sognarti,

Son felice di sbagliarmi,

Johanna!

In the Winter 2001 issue, we published a story about the production of *Pacific Overtures* that later was brought to Washington for the Kennedy Center Sondheim Celebration. In an article he wrote for us, Gary Perlman, a Tokyo-based writer and producer, noted the challenges of translating English to Japanese.

"Due to the peculiarities of Japanese pronunciation," he wrote, "words and phrases tend to be longer than their English counterparts; for example, 'Sondheim' in Japanese is six syllables. Since each syllable must be represented by one note, the result is some very long musical phrases, meaning that only about half the information in an English song can be conveyed in Japanese. Given the amount of information packed into a typical Sondheim song, the translator is often hard-pressed just to convey the story, never mind characterization or poetry."

Here is the start of "Poems" as translated by Kuni Hashimoto.

English original

Rain glistening

On the silver birch,

Like my lady's tears.

Your turn.

Rain gathering,

Winding into streams,

Like the roads to Boston.
Your turn.

Japanese Translation

Ame oto ni
Kokoro furuwase
Tsuma wa matsu
(Kotae yo)

America to
Hibiki ga niteru
Ame no oto
(Dohzo)

In The Netherlands, Allard Blom did the translations for a tour of *Company* by the Musical Theater Division of the Royal Ballet of Flanders, and we covered it in the Winter 2000 issue.

"Sondheim's lyrics are extremely compact," Blom wrote. "He is one of the few lyricists who never says too little and never says too much. This makes the translation of his work an almost impossible task. The opening title song (of *Company*), for instance, was a problem. In Dutch, there is no word for 'company,' so I translated it into a word that means 'with each other.'

"Everybody thought that I would have sleepless nights over 'Not Getting Married Today.' Honestly, this was one of the numbers that frightened me when I started working on the show, but it turned out to be a breeze compared to some other numbers. The joy in 'Not Getting

Married' is that the fast lyrics don't need to rhyme. So, as a translator, you just focus on the richness of the humor within the lyrics."

Here's a brief translation of "You Could Drive a Person Crazy":

But worse than that
A person that
Titillates a person and then leaves her flat

This became:

Maaar wat ik haat
Wat echt niet gaat
Is iemand die je opgeilt
En dan liggen laten

Which would literally be:

But what I hate
What is really impossible
Is someone who turns you on
And then leaves you.

When Ulricha Johnson translated *Into the Woods* into Swedish for the Sodra Teatern in Stockholm (Winter 1999), she said, "Sondheim's work has substance. There's always layers of meaning under what he writes. That way, if I can't translate the lyrics literally, I try to think about what he's really trying to say and get the meaning in some other way.

"Like in 'I Know Things Now,' Red Ridinghood sings, *'Take extra care with strangers/Even flowers have their dangers.'* That became

Tro inte gott om alla (Don't think well of everyone)
I en falla kan man falla (You might fall in a trap)

In Helsinki, the Finnish National Opera's *Sweeney Todd* played to sold-out crowds in a huge auditorium (Winter 1998). Finnish is one of the most difficult languages in the world, and Sondheim's lyrics must have posed an enormous challenge for the translator, Juice Leskinen, a pop music icon and songwriter. While some of the wit and elusive quality of the original was lost, his version retained its spirit amazingly well. For example, there was this translation of *'Lift your razor high, Sweeney/Hear it singing, 'Yes!'/Sink it in the rosy skin/Of righteousness!':*

Veitses heilahtaa, Sweeney!
Kauas taivaisiin!
Virtaa verta joka kerta viemariin!

Claudio Botelho is an actor, singer, director, and composer/lyricist who played Robert in *Company* in Rio de Janiero—he also translated the whole show into Portuguese. He talked about the translation challenges in our Summer 2001 issue.

"First of all, the rhymes. Where Sondheim has chosen unusual rhymes such as 'dollar' and 'Mahler,' or internal rhymes like 'if you're quick/for a kick/you could pick...', one would expect the translation to present similar rhymes in the new language. And *Company* is full of those tricks in rhyme and rhythm.

"Another point is the sound of the words. Two classic songs of the show, 'The Ladies Who Lunch' and 'Being Alive,' each end with the same sound, an open vowel. Even if we wanted to translate this part literally, no such sound exists in Portuguese. And the performer would need that open sound for the high notes in both songs. So that's why, in many circumstances, this translator had to adapt the song so that it could have not only the original sense but also a similar sound that could carry the music."

This was his translation of the final section of "Being Alive":

Somebody crowd me with love,
Somebody force me to care,
Somebody let me come through,
I'll always be there
As frightened as you,
To help us survive
Being alive, being alive, being alive.

Alguém me enchendo de amor
Alguém jurando esquecer
Alguém me dando o que tem
Tentando entender
Com medo também
Que a vida é mais
Viver é mais, viver é mais, viver é mais

Is something lost in translation in these productions? Of course. But the story and the meanings are still there—and so is the music and whole new worlds to think about. And the unthinkable alternative would be not to present Sondheim at all.

There's also something about hearing a Sondheim song in one's own language. Consider, for example, the following opening lines from *Company's* "Barcelona" that were translated into Catalan and sung—where else? in Barcelona (Summer 1997).

> *Robert: On te'n vas?*
> *April: A Barcelona.*
> *Robert: …ah…*
> *April: Pots dormir!*
> *Robert: Has de ferho?*
> *April: He d'anarhi.*
> *Robert: …ah…*

Needless to say, everyone knew what was going on between Robert and April, and the song brought down the house.

FROM *Gold!* TO BOUNCE

THE SONDHEIM WORLD was holding its breath in 2003. Finally, the Mizner musical, with music and lyrics by Stephen Sondheim and a book by John Weidman, would hit the stage. *Gold!* (the new name for *Wise Guys*) would have its world premiere at the Goodman Theater in Chicago in June with Hal Prince directing. I called Sondheim and, just as he had been with *Passion*, he was excited to talk about this new show.

"There will be some major changes from the workshop," he said. "In fact, about a third of the score has been rewritten. We'll have a new opening number, not the title song from *Wise Guys*. That's because the show isn't about wise guys anymore.

"What we called the 'New York Sequence' has been expanded in the first act, and we've added material to the 'Boca Raton Sequence.' Papa Mizner's song 'It's In Your Hands Now' has been changed because of the new thrust of the show, which is more on American enterprise and reinvention and not so much about the brothers and their mother.

"John and I have also added a leading female character. Hal wanted that. Basically, he said we need more sex. Actually, I had a leading female character in the outline for the show that I did in 1952.

"I should also say that the show is swift and sharp. It's a real musical comedy. When you've got Addison and Wilson Mizner traveling from California to Alaska to New York to Florida, it has to be a romp through America.

"But the structure of the show is exactly the same as in the workshop. The difference is in tone, and that's what made Hal want to do this."

Sondheim gave us permission to publish the lyrics to three of the songs: "Gold!," "Isn't He Something" and "Talent." Here are brief excerpts.

GOLD!

Prospector:

Gold! Go to Dawson City, boys!

It isn't very pretty,

But it's get rich quick!

Found me a motherlode,

Warn't no trick!

Wanna find another lode!

Dig in any mountain.

Pan in any crick!

All you need's a bucket

And a shovel and a pick

And with a little bit of luck it

Means you get rich quick!

ISN'T HE SOMETHING?

Mama:

Seldom comes to see me,

Hardly ever calls.

When he sends me letters,

They're just two-line scrawls.

Isn't he something?
Things he says out loud I wouldn't dare,
Or I'd have to hide.
Skates along through life without a care
Or a shred of pride.
But look at him glide!
Isn't he something!
See how he glides.

He's having the time of his life,
Life filled to the brim.
And I've had the time of my life,
Living through him.
Some men are tender souls
With worthy goals.
They keep fulfilling.
Some men ignore the rules,
Are rogues and fools,
And thrilling.

TALENT

Hollis:
I had this dream of becoming an artist—
A painter, a poet, who knows?
I had a nice little talent for drawing,
And a natural feeling for prose.
I even began to compose.

So many talents,
Wasn't I blest!
All of them good,
A few of them better,
None of them best,
Just enough talent to know
That I hadn't the talent,
So I put my dream
And my self-esteem
To rest.

Even before the Chicago opening and after the advertising had gone out, however, the name of the show was changed from *Gold!* to *Bounce,* and that was the title of the opening song at the Goodman in Chicago. With Hal Prince directing, the show starred Richard Kind as Addison and Howard McGillin as Wilson Mizner. Petite movie star Jane Powell was their mother, and Gavin Creel was Hollis.

Although the critics liked some of Sondheim's score, they gave the show very mixed reviews:

The *Chicago Tribune*: "The problem with world-class talents is more our problem than theirs. We expect the world of them, every time. Stephen Sondheim is a world-class talent. He has the right to do a modest, unpretentious show whenever he likes.

"But the wit, melodic spice, and stylistic brinksmanship distinguishing Sondheim's music theater career, across hugely important shows and minor ones, leave you unprepared for the dispiriting mildness of *Bounce,* Sondheim's first new show since *Passion* nine years ago.…"

"The show lacks its titular ingredient. It's not edgy enough in its love/hate brotherly dynamics and exploration in American rapaciousness, and it's not funny enough to be a full-bodied musical comedy. It's eh. And if there's one reaction I thought I'd never have to a new Sondheim musical, it's eh."

Chicago Sun-Times: "Can all these grand themes be shoehorned into a picaresque musical that seems to want to recapture the nifty bounce of *A Funny Thing Happened on the Way to the Forum* on the one hand, while suggesting the gravity of the Sondheim-Weidman collaboration *Assassins* on the other? Yes and no. Tone is a big problem in *Bounce,* and one that director Harold Prince has not fully resolved."

So it was back to the drawing boards before moving the musical to Washington in the fall.

SONDHEIM ON *Bounce*

D URING PREVIEWS of *Bounce* at the Kennedy Center in Washington, Sondheim, John Weidman, and Jonathan Tunick gave separate interviews about the show. Mark Eden Horowitz taped them. This is the section in which Sondheim participated.

Sondheim: "When I first started the show—130 years ago—I was interested in Wilson, and Addison was part of the story. John was interested in the symbiotic relationship of the brothers.

"I've never written this many shows to get to one show. We've had four distinct scripts and scores for this show. Some of the songs were obviously retained and even some moments in the scenes—although I dare say if you went to John Weidman's first draft and then compared it to this draft, my guess is there's probably less than two or three pages that are in common.

"There are two or three, maybe four songs that have lasted. Oddly enough, the sequence of events has remained the same, because it's a historical piece. And the first draft, though it was interrupted by a number of vaudeville numbers, started out in Benecia, California, and went to the Gold Rush, and went to New York, and then went to Florida. That structure was always there. So even when a number would be replaced, it would be in a similar spot."

Early songs and drafts of the script envisioned the show presented in a vaudeville style.

Sondheim: "John pointed out when we got the vaudeville idea, that coincidentally vaudeville started in the 1880s and died in the 1930s, and the Mizners started in the 1880s and died in the 1930s. And so it was curiously appropriate, although that wasn't the reason that we chose to do it that way."

Although that vision of the show changed, there are still vestiges in the design and score, notably the song "Bounce."

Sondheim: "As it is now, there's only one vaudeville number in the show, which opens and closes the first act and closes the second act. It's the title number."

Speaking more specifically about the style of the score, Sondheim said: "It's a 1950s score in the sense that it's primarily in eight, sixteen, and thirty-two bar chunks. Many of the songs are in fact thirty-two bar songs, or variations thereof, in AABA or ABAB form.

"The harmonic language is, again, a kind of very tonal language with moderately simple key relationships that I was writing in the late '50s (not on Broadway) and when I was writing things like *Forum*, which is early '60s—what I was recapturing when I did *Merrily We Roll Along*. It's that kind of a score—it's a *Merrily We Roll Along* kind of score. I wanted it to be crisp and bright and simple and direct, with primary colors, because we first started to write the show in a rather cartoony style, a Hope-Crosby kind of musical like the 'road pictures.' Swiftness is a major element—not that all songs are fast, but all the songs make their point and get off. At least that's the intention. There are very few extended pieces in it.

"The audiences enjoyed it in Chicago. And they particularly enjoyed it by the end of the run. We all left immediately after we opened. By the time John and I got back, two months later, at the end of the summer, the performances were sure-footed and the audience always smells that. The problem was we had no rehearsal time in Chicago after the opening because of the limitations of the budget. So there was no point in rewriting while we were in Chicago, because there was no time to rehearse it. All we could do is what we did, which is get it in as good shape as we could by opening night."

In the interviews, Sondheim and Weidman both seemed confident in describing the changes they felt were needed, most of which focused on what they referred to as the New York sequence and the Boca Raton sequence.

But even before that, according to Sondheim: "I thought the most important scene to fix, or moment to fix, was the scene with Papa's death—the one that starts the show off. Because that's usually where a show gets in trouble, right at the beginning. The opening number worked fine, but as soon as the story started, you didn't know what the story was about. The way the first scene was written and, particularly the way it was performed in Chicago, you didn't even know what kind of show you were in for, because the father was played as a completely comic-strip character, whereas the mother and the boys were not. So you're off on the wrong foot already.

"Now it's all of a piece, and it makes a huge difference. There has been a little rewriting of the scene, but very little. I cut about a quarter of the song and took out the silly things I had in there—the father saying 'tooneropity' when he meant 'opportunity,' because his mind is going, all that kind of stuff. It's all decoration. It's what George Kaufman said:

'Take out the improvements.' You know, take out everything that isn't necessary. And that's what we did. And as far as I'm concerned, that makes more difference to the show than anything else we did.

"We all looked at each other on Sunday after we put in most of the changes to the Boca Raton sequence, and thought: This is the show we mean."

The cast was the same when the show moved from Chicago to Washington, but even after changes were made, the reviews were again mixed to negative.

The New York Times: "Somehow *Bounce*, directed by the mighty Harold Prince, never seems to leave its starting point. The map lies tantalizingly before you, its routes and destinations marked in bright colors. But it remains a wistful diagram, rarely closer to three dimensions than the outsized, hand-tinted tourist postcards that frame the set. It's like a travel agent's pitch for a wondrous vacation...."

"Much of the music, while whispering of earlier, more flashily complex Sondheim scores, has a conventional surface perkiness that suggests a more old-fashioned, crowd-pleasing kind of show than is this composer's wont. But his extraordinary gift for stealthily weaving dark motifs into a brighter musical fabric is definitely in evidence, mellifluously rendered in the peerless Jonathan Tunick's orchestrations."

The Washington Post: 'The Florida sequence, culminating in 'Get Rich Quick,' which may be the first production-number salute to real estate, comes as a relief in *Bounce* on two counts. It shows that Sondheim is still an improvisatory wizard with the show tune; the masterly use of lyric to mimic dialogue is at times wonderful. And, to some minor degree, it mitigates the disappointment in virtually all that has come before it. Remember that we are now two hours into *Bounce,* and painful as it is to report, the scenes in Florida are the first indication of any theatrical spark in the show. What precedes them is a wan and dramatically shallow musical comedy, the surprisingly uninvolving tale of the rivalry between a mismatched pair of siblings."

(On November 18, 2008, the musical, now titled *Road Show*, surfaced at the Public Theater off-Broadway with John Doyle directing. Rewritten without an intermission and without the leading female character of Nellie, it starred Michael Cerveris as Wilson and Alexander Gemignani as Addison Mizner, Alma Cuervo as Mama and Claybourne Elder as Hollis. Again, the reviews were not favorable. *The New York Times* said: "The problem is that this musical's travelogue structure precludes its digging deep. It hints at dark and shimmering glories beneath the surface that it never fully mines. Like its leading characters, *Road Show* doesn't quite know what to do with the riches at its disposal.")

Moving ON

B Y EARLY 2004, I had edited *The Sondheim Review* for ten years. We had covered the Broadway opening of Sondheim's newest show, *Passion;* the world premiere in London of his earliest, *Saturday Night*; and the tortuous journey of the Mizner musical, from *Wise Guys* to *Gold!* to its Chicago and Washington premieres when it was called *Bounce*. We had covered the Broadway revivals of *Company, A Funny Thing Happened on the Way to the Forum, Follies, Into the Woods*, and *Gypsy*. We had covered his flop murder mystery, *Getting Away with Murder*. We had covered tributes and interviews and the enormous Kennedy Center Sondheim Celebration. The magazine had grown in size, substance, and variety.

I was extremely proud of the work of our reporters, writers, and editors. Because of their (mostly unpaid) efforts, I think the magazine was informative, interesting, and, some would say indispensable for Sondheim followers. As per its initial intention, it was never a fanzine or a scholarly journal but simply journalism, filled with news, interviews, reviews, essays, photos, book and CD reviews, and much more. It was, as I had promised at the start, always about the work and not the man.

Besides assigning stories, guiding our writers and editors ,and supervising the design and printing of the magazine, I had traveled considerably for it. To New York for the Broadway revivals, to Washington for the Kennedy Center productions, to London for *Saturday Night*, to Chicago and Washington for *Bounce*.

And just because I wanted to see other Sondheim shows, I went to Milburn, N.J., for Paper Mill's *Follies*, to Ravinia for *Night Music*, to Chicago's Lyric Opera for *Sweeney* with Bryn Terfel, to Los Angeles for *Assassins*, to Dallas for *The Frogs*, to Ann Arbor for the concert by the "younger selves" in *Follies*, to Philadelphia for *Passion*, to Birmingham, Ala., for *Passion*. I was one of the few to see *Getting Away with Murder* in New York.

And I knew there was still more Sondheim to come. Our 10th anniversary issue (Spring 2004) would announce that Nathan Lane had expanded *The Frogs*, and it would play at Lincoln Center starting in July. (Sondheim expanded the score from six songs to thirteen, but the show received mixed reviews and closed after 92 performances.)

Also, *Assassins* would finally make it to Broadway, opening in March at Studio 54 with Neil Patrick Harris as both the Balladeer and Lee Harvey Oswald, the roles he would have played if the production had not been canceled in 2001 because of 9/11. (The show ran for 101 performances and won five Tony awards, including best revival of a musical.)

It seemed like there would always be a Sondheim show somewhere, but it was time for me, in the words of one of his songs, to "move on." I sent a note to Sondheim saying that the Spring 2004 issue would be my last as editor. I received a one-sentence acknowledgment.

February 25, 2004

Dear Paul –

Thanks for your note, and all your devotion over the years.

Best,

Steve

Some people have asked if I was expecting a more effusive farewell. No. Sondheim and I had always had a journalist-source relationship, and I didn't expect anything more.

My assistant editor took the magazine over and it continued until 2016, when it folded. An online follow-up, *Everything Sondheim*, lasted a year.

In 2011, my wife and I moved to a smaller apartment and I had to find a home for my large collection of Sondheim DVDs, CDs, cassette tapes, videotapes, books, programs, clippings—along with the notes, letters, and faxes. I donated it all to the Marquette University Memorial Library, which established the Stephen Sondheim Research Collection. It is available to the public.

I received three notes from Sondheim after I left the magazine. One said he thought it was a good idea to give my collection to Marquette, and another thanked me for a DVD I sent (I can't remember what it was).

The third was written after I had given a talk about Sondheim to a local Jewish organization. An audience member wondered if and how Sondheim's Jewish heritage influenced his work. I didn't have an answer, so I asked him.

April 8, 2015

Dear Paul –

Thanks for the note – and early birthday congratulations.

As for your talk, I have nothing to say about my Jewish heritage as an influence on my work. I was brought up as a secular Jew and was never even in a temple until I was 21 and attended a friend's bar mitzvah.

As always,

Steve

REMEMBERING *the Legend*

L IKE SO MANY OTHERS, I was shocked and saddened when I heard of Sondheim's unexpected death on November 26, 2021. Although I had taken a totally different personal path after my editorship and began writing novels set in Tuscany, which I continue to do, *The Sondheim Review* and my connection to Stephen Sondheim had remained a major part of my life. I no longer went to New York to see his shows, but I did see local productions, and I enjoyed reading the frequent articles about the awards, the interviews, the progress on his next show.

I thought back to the odd roles I had for ten years. I was a journalist first, and my goal for *The Sondheim Review* was always that it serve as an informative journal covering Sondheim's works. My main source, of course, was Sondheim himself. I was on a first name basis with an acknowledged genius, the winner of seven Tony awards, a Pulitzer, an Oscar, eight Grammys, the Presidential Medal of Freedom, etc. etc. etc. who wrote me notes and letters and called to give me information as a journalist.

But I was also a tremendous fan, starting when I saw *Follies* in 1972 (I still am). I loved going to his shows, some of them multiple times. I tried, not always successfully, I admit, to keep the roles separate.

When I reviewed his letters and notes, I found that, yes, from thousands and thousands of words in each issue, Sondheim could find an "emendation" about a wrong name or misspelling. But I knew that he often used those notes to provide new insights into the background of a character, a scene, or a show—things I hadn't known about.

Although we had upset him with our review of the London *Passion* and irritated him by printing his "juvenilia," Sondheim's letters, notes, and faxes were almost always informative, forthcoming, encouraging, and sometimes even enthusiastic. "Congratulations." "Everything seems kosher." "Keep up the good work." "Best." "As always." Throughout my ten years as editor, he answered my questions promptly and thoroughly.

I often wondered how he felt when new issues arrived. Because he apparently read every word in *The Sondheim Review,* at least at the beginning, I have a feeling that he enjoyed learning details of the productions of his shows in the U.S. and around the world. How else would he have known about *Assassins* in Tel Aviv, *A Little Night Music* in Munich, *Pacific Overtures* in Sydney, *Company* in Vienna?

I imagine he liked to read our interviews with the stars of his shows, remembering not just Bernadette Peters, Glynis Johns, Elaine Stritch, and Mandy Patinkin, but also people like Kelsey Grammer (*Sweeney Todd*), Michael Hayden (*Merrily We Roll Along*), Marge Champion (*Follies*), Claire Bloom (*A Little Night Music*), Leslie Uggams (*Into the Woods*), and Lynn Redgrave (*Company*).

Settling back in his leather chair, Blacking pencil in hand, he may have examined page by page, word by word, our reports of his less frequently performed musicals: *Saturday Night, Anyone Can Whistle, Do I Hear a Waltz?, Pacific Overtures, The Frogs.*

Reading their profiles and interviews, he must have remembered (fondly, I hope) working with Paul Gemignani, Paul Ford, Hal Prince, Scott Ellis, Jonathan Tunick, John Weidman, Paul McKibbins, and Michael Starobin.

I suspect that if he could have met with the authors, he would have argued the fine points in their essays on such topics as *Assassins* as a discourse on democracy in America; Freud's influence on *Into the Woods;* the role of dance in his musicals; the role of the "outsider" in his works; his use of musical repetition to underscore obsession.

I think he would have enjoyed the puzzles and contests.

This all brought back so many memories for me. In a way, those years feel like a long time ago, and in another way, they feel like yesterday. I thought back to the very first time Sondheim called. He was so excited about *Passion* because for him every new show was a new challenge and a new adventure. I think he was like George in *Sunday:*

> *I want to move on*
> *I want to explore the light*
> *I want to know how to get through*
> *Through to something new*
> *Something of my own*

I wrote a letter to *The New York Times* about our first conversation. It was published five days after his death.

To the Editor:

As a journalist and longtime fan of Stephen Sondheim's works, I had a crazy idea in 1994: I would start a magazine devoted to his works.

I didn't need his permission, but I wrote him a letter. To my surprise, he called me on a Sunday afternoon. He said the idea was fine, though he didn't think there would be much to put in a magazine.

We then talked for three hours about the show he was writing: *Passion*. He asked if I had seen the Italian film on which it was based, *Passione d'Amore*. I had not. The next week, a videotape of the film arrived in the mail. That's the kind of man Stephen Sondheim was.

Paul Salsini

Milwaukee

The writer is the founder and former editor of *The Sondheim Review*.

A CHRONOLOGY

Unless noted, all music and lyrics are by Stephen Sondheim (SS).

March 22, 1930
Stephen Joshua Sondheim is born in New York City to
Janet Fox and Herbert Sondheim

1937
SS begins piano lessons

1940
SS's parents divorce and he moves with his mother to rural
Pennsylvania, where he becomes acquainted with the neighbors,
Oscar Hammerstein II and family

1942
SS enters the George School in Newtown, Pa.

1945
SS and friends write the school musical *By George*

1946
SS enters Williams College in Williamstown, Mass.,
intending to major in mathematics

1947

During his summer vacation, SS serves as a gofer on the set of
Rodgers and Hammerstein's *Allegro*

May 1948

Phinney's Rainbow is performed at Williams College

March 1949

All That Glitters is performed at Williams College

1950

SS graduates from Williams magna cum laude and
receives the Hutchinson Prize, which allows him to
study under Milton Babbitt

1953

SS is the clapper boy during the filming in Italy of
John Huston's *Beat the Devil*

1953-54

SS writes episodes for the CBS television series *Topper*

1954

A television musical adaptation of Frank Stockton's
The Lady or the Tiger? written with Mary Rodgers is abandoned

1955

SS's first Broadway effort, *Saturday Night*,
is abandoned when the producer dies

1956

SS writes the incidental music for the Broadway production
The Girls of Summer

1956

Another Broadway musical attempt,
The Last Resorts, is scrapped

1956

SS is chosen to write the lyrics for *West Side Story*
with music by Leonard Bernstein

September 26, 1957

West Side Story (music by Leonard Bernstein;
book by Arthur Laurents) opens on Broadway

1958

SS is asked to write the songs for Arthur Laurents' book of
Gypsy; at Ethel Merman's request, another composer,
Jule Styne, is brought in, so SS writes lyrics only

May 21, 1959

Gypsy (music by Jule Styne; book by Arthur Laurents)
starring Ethel Merman opens on Broadway

November 1959

SS with Jule Styne is nominated for (but doesn't win)
the Grammy Award for Song of the Year for
"Small World" from *Gypsy*

SONDHEIM & Me

1960

SS writes the incidental music for Arthur Laurents'
play *Invitation to a March*

October 1961

Robert Wise and Jerome Robbins' film of
West Side Story is released, winning ten Academy Awards
(but none for its principal creators)

May 8, 1962

The first Broadway production with lyrics AND music by SS,
A Funny Thing Happened on the Way to the Forum
(book by Burt Shevelove and Larry Gelbart),
opens on Broadway starring Zero Mostel

1963

Forum wins the Tony Award for best musical,
the first of many for SS

April 4 - 11, 1964

Anyone Can Whistle with a book by Arthur Laurents has nine
performances on Broadway. It stars Angela Lansbury,
Lee Remick, and Harry Guardino

March 18, 1965

Do I Hear a Waltz? (music by Richard Rodgers;
book by Arthur Laurents) opens on Broadway
starring Elizabeth Allen and Sergio Franchi

1965

SS and James Goldman begin work on *The Girls Upstairs*,
which eventually evolves into *Follies* (1971)

1966

Richard Lester's film of *A Funny Thing Happened on the Way to the Forum* is released (without most of Sondheim's songs)

November 16, 1966

A one-hour musical drama *Evening Primrose* (four songs by SS; teleplay by James Goldman) is telecast on ABC

December 11, 1966

SS and Lee Remick appear as a celebrity guest team on an episode of the game show *Password* on CBS. They play opposite Peter Lawford and Audrey Meadows

1968

The Exception and the Rule, aka *A Pray by Blecht*, a musical with music by Leonard Bernstein and lyrics by SS, is abandoned

1968 - 1969

SS's crossword puzzles appear in *New York Magazine*

1969

Harold Prince agrees to produce *The Girls Upstairs* after SS agrees to help with a series of playlets by George Furth, which eventually becomes *Company*

April 26, 1970

Company, with book by George Furth and starring Dean Jones and Elaine Stritch, opens on Broadway and wins the Tony Award for Best Musical. This and all new SS Broadway productions through 1981 are directed by Harold Prince

1970

Documentary filmmaker D. A. Pennebaker releases *Original Cast Album: Company*, a film about the recording of the show

March 16, 1971

SS wins his first Grammy Award for Best Score from an Original Cast Show Album for *Company*

April 4, 1971

Follies with a book by James Goldman opens on Broadway starring Alexis Smith, Gene Nelson, Dorothy Collins, John McMartin, and Yvonne De Carlo

April 4, 1972

A revival of *A Funny Thing Happened on the Way to the Forum* opens on Broadway with Phil Silvers as Pseudolus

February 25, 1973

A Little Night Music (book by Hugh Wheeler) opens on Broadway starring Glynis Johns, Len Cariou, and Hermione Gingold. For an unprecedented third year in a row, SS wins the Tony Award for Best Score of a Musical

March 11, 1973

A benefit concert honoring SS is performed on the set of *A Little Night Music*, released as *Sondheim: A Musical Tribute*

April 23, 1973

SS appears on the cover of *Newsweek*

1973

The film *The Last of Sheila* is released with a screenplay
by SS and Anthony Perkins

1974

The first edition of *Sondheim & Co.*, Craig Zadan's
biography of SS, is published

January 30, 1974

SS appears in a supporting role in a television production
of the Kaufman-Lardner play *June Moon*

March 10, 1974

Harold Prince's revival of Leonard Bernstein's *Candide*
with lyrical revisions by SS opens on Broadway

May 20, 1974

The Frogs (book and direction by Burt Shevelove)
is performed in the Yale Swimming Pool

September 23, 1974

A revival of *Gypsy* starring Angela Lansbury opens on Broadway

December 1974

Alain Resnais' film *Stavisky* with a score by SS is released

July 26, 1975

Judy Collins' recording of "Send in the Clowns"
enters the Billboard Top 40 chart

January 11, 1976

Pacific Overtures with a book by John Weidman
opens on Broadway starring Mako as The Reciter

February 28, 1976

SS wins the Grammy Award for Song of the Year for
"Send in the Clowns"

April 18, 1977

Side by Side by Sondheim, a musical revue directed by
Ned Sherrin, moves from London to Broadway

March 1978

Harold Prince's film of *A Little Night Music* is released

March 1, 1979

Sweeney Todd with a book by Hugh Wheeler opens on Broadway
starring Len Cariou and Angela Lansbury and wins the Tony
Award for Best Musical

February 14, 1980

A revival of *West Side Story* opens on Broadway

October 29, 1980

Marry Me a Little, a musical revue of obscure and/or discarded
songs by SS (conceived by Craig Lucas and Norman Rene),
opens off-Broadway

November 16 - 28, 1981

Merrily We Roll Along (book by George Furth)
has 16 performances on Broadway; the Harold Prince / SS
partnership comes to an end

December 1981

Warren Beatty's film *Reds* is released with a score by SS

March 23, 1983

Concerts in honor of SS are performed at Sotheby Parke Bernet
in New York and released as *A Stephen Sondheim Evening*

July 6, 1983

Workshop performances of
Sunday in the Park with George begin

May 2, 1984

Sunday in the Park with George (book and direction by
James Lapine) opens on Broadway starring Mandy Patinkin
and Bernadette Peters

October 25, 1984

A revised *Pacific Overtures* opens off-Broadway with a cast
featuring Ernest Abuba and Kevin Gray

April 14, 1985

SS and James Lapine are awarded the Pulitzer Prize for
Sunday in the Park with George

June 16, 1985

A revised version of *Merrily We Roll Along* directed by
James Lapine opens in San Diego

September 6-7, 1985

All-star concert performances of *Follies* are performed at Lincoln
Center in New York and released as *Follies in Concert*

November 18, 1985
Barbra Streisand's *The Broadway Album* is released,
with eight SS songs (three with lyrical revision by SS).
It hits #1 on the Billboard album chart

December 4, 1986
Workshop performances of *Into the Woods* with book and
direction by James Lapine begin in San Diego

July 21, 1987
A major revision of *Follies* with new songs by SS and a revised
book by James Goldman opens in London

November 5, 1987
Into the Woods opens on Broadway starring Bernadette Peters,
Joanna Gleason, Chip Zien, and Kim Crosby

September 14, 1989
The first Broadway revival of *Sweeney Todd* opens at the Circle in
the Square starring Bob Gunton and Beth Fowler

November 16, 1989
A revival of *Gypsy* starring Tyne Daly opens on Broadway and
wins the Tony Award for Best Revival of a Musical

March 15, 1990
The first London production of *Sunday in the Park with George*
opens with Philip Quast as George and Maria Friedman as Dot

June 15, 1990
Warren Beatty's film *Dick Tracy* is released with five songs by SS

November 7, 1990
PBS telecasts the New York City Opera's production of
A Little Night Music starring Sally Ann Howes,
George Lee Andrews, and Regina Resnick

December 18, 1990
Assassins with a book by John Weidman opens off-Broadway
featuring a cast that includes Victor Garber, Terrence Mann,
and Patrick Cassidy

1991
SS wins the Academy Award for Best Song for
"Sooner or Later" from *Dick Tracy*

June 10, 1992
A benefit concert honoring SS is performed at Carnegie Hall
and released as *Sondheim: A Celebration at Carnegie Hall*

April 1, 1993
Putting It Together, a musical revue imported from London and
starring Julie Andrews, opens off-Broadway at the Manhattan
Theater Club

March / April 1993
Original cast reunion concerts of *Company* are performed

December 5, 1993
SS is a recipient of the Kennedy Center Honors

December 12, 1993
A filmed version of *Gypsy* starring
Bette Midler is televised on CBS

May 9, 1994
Passion with book and direction by James Lapine opens on
Broadway starring Donna Murphy, Jere Shea, and Marin Mazzie
and wins the Tony Award for Best Musical

May 15, 1994
Tenth anniversary reunion concert of
Sunday in the Park with George is performed

May 26, 1994
The revised *Merrily We Roll Along* opens at the
York Theater in New York

June 1994
The first issue of *The Sondheim Review* is published

April 8, 1995
An all-star benefit concert performance of
Anyone Can Whistle is recorded

1995
The Kennedy Center announces that it has commissioned SS
and John Weidman to write a musical, tentatively titled *Wise
Guys* and based on the lives of the Mizner brothers, a project SS
has had on the back burner for forty years

February 24, 1995
A fire at his townhouse destroys supplies and records
and kills his Standard Poodle Max

October 5, 1995
The first major New York revival of *Company* opens on
Broadway starring Boyd Gaines and Debra Monk. Plans to
move to a larger house in December are scrapped

March 8, 1996
Mike Nichols' film *The Birdcage* is released
with three songs by SS

March 17, 1996
After a tryout in San Diego, *Getting Away With Murder*,
a play by SS and George Furth, opens on Broadway and
closes after 17 performances

April 18, 1996
A smash hit revival of *A Funny Thing Happened on the Way to the
Forum* starring Nathan Lane opens on Broadway

January 9, 1997
SS accepts the National Medal of Arts from the
National Endowment for the Arts

November 9, 1997
Benefit concerts of *Into the Woods* are performed on
Broadway by the original cast to commemorate the
tenth anniversary of the show

December 17, 1997
More than 40 years after it was written, the first full production
of *Saturday Night* opens at the Bridewell Theater in London

June 1998
Stephen Sondheim: A Life, a major biography by
Meryle Secrest, is published

March 12-14, 1999
Concert performances of *Sweeney Todd* are presented in
Los Angeles to commemorate its twentieth anniversary.
Kelsey Grammer and Christine Baranski star

May 19, 1999
The American premiere of *Saturday Night* is
produced by Chicago's Pegasus Players

October 29, 1999
A workshop of *Wise Guys* is presented by the New York Theater
Workshop. Nathan Lane and Victor Garber star

November 21, 1999
A new production of *Putting It Together* opens on
Broadway starring Carol Burnett

February 17, 2000
The New York premiere of *Saturday Night* begins at the
Second Stage Theater

May 4-6, 2000

Three concert performances of *Sweeney Todd* are presented
by the New York Philharmonic to celebrate Sondheim's 70th
birthday. Starring Bryn Terfel and Emma Thompson, the
concerts are recorded by and broadcast on PBS

May 22, 2000

The Library of Congress celebrates Sondheim's birthday
with a concert in Washington

December 11, 2000

The West End premiere of *Merrily We Roll Along* opens at
the Donmar Warehouse with a cast led by Julian Ovenden,
Samantha Spiro, and Daniel Evans

April 5, 2001

The first Broadway revival of *Follies* opens with Blythe Danner,
Treat Williams, Judith Ivey, Gregory Harrison, and Polly Bergen
in the cast. It closes on July 14, 2001

July 19-21, 2001

Three concerts of *Sweeney Todd* are presented by the
San Francisco Symphony and later shown on PBS.
George Hearn and Patti LuPone star

September 13, 2001

Plans for the first Broadway production of *Assassins*,
originally scheduled for November, are scrapped due to
the tragic events of September 11, 2001

October 16, 2001

The world premiere recording of the score
from *The Frogs* is released

April 30, 2002

A new production of *Into the Woods* opens on Broadway with a
cast headed by Vanessa Williams and John McMartin

May 10, 2002

The opening night performance of *Sweeney Todd*
begins a four-month Sondheim Celebration at the
Kennedy Center in Washington

July 9, 2002

A limited engagement of Amon Miyamoto's Japanese-language
version of *Pacific Overtures* opens at Lincoln Center in New York
and then plays at the Kennedy Center in Washington

May 1, 2003

Another revival of *Gypsy*, this time starring
Bernadette Peters, opens on Broadway

June 30, 2003

The world premiere of *Bounce*, originally called
Wise Guys and then *Gold!*, takes place at the Goodman Theater
in Chicago. Hal Prince is the director and it stars
Richard Kind and Howard McGillin

October 30, 2003

The Kennedy Center production of *Bounce* opens
at the Eisenhower Theatre in Washington

April 22, 2004

The first Broadway production of *Assassins* begins at Studio 54 directed by Joe Mantello and with Neil Patrick Harris and Michael Cerveris in the cast

July 22, 2004

A revised and expanded production of *The Frogs*, adapted by Nathan Lane and with several new songs by SS, opens at Lincoln Center

October 20, 2004

Most of the original Broadway cast of *Passion* return for a Tenth Anniversary Concert

December 2, 2004

A Broadway revival of *Pacific Overtures* opens at Studio 54. It is an English-language version by Amon Miyamoto's New National Theater

March 2005

Several tribute concerts are performed to celebrate SS's 75th birthday, including *Wall to Wall Stephen Sondheim* on March 19, *Children and Art* on March 21, and *Stephen Sondheim's 75th: The Concert* on July 8

March 30-April 1, 2005

A semi-staged concert of *Passion* starring Patti LuPone, Michael Cerveris, and Audra McDonald is held at Lincoln Center and broadcast by PBS

SONDHEIM & Me

May 10, 2005

Stephen Sondheim Sings, the first volume of SS demos performed by the composer, is released on PS Classics.
A second volume appears in October

November 3, 2005

A revival of *Sweeney Todd* opens on Broadway directed by John Doyle, with the actors playing their own instruments. Michael Cerveris and Patti LuPone star

November 29, 2006

A Broadway revival of *Company* opens with Raul Esparza as Bobby and Barbara Walsh as Joanne. It is directed by John Doyle and the actors play their own instruments

February 8-12, 2007

Encores! presents a concert version of *Follies* at New York City Center starring Donna Murphy, Victoria Clark, Victor Garber, Michael McGrath, and Christine Baranski

March 4, 2007

An animated SS voiced by the man himself appears on an episode of the television series *The Simpsons*

July 9-29, 2007

Encores! at New York City Center presents a concert version of *Gypsy* starring Patti LuPone

December 21, 2007

The film version of *Sweeney Todd*, directed by
Tim Burton, opens in theaters. It stars Johnny Depp
and Helena Bonham Carter

February 21, 2008

The 2006 London revival of *Sunday in the Park With George*
transfers to New York's Studio 54, becoming the show's first
Broadway revival. It stars Daniel Evans and Jenna Russell

March 27, 2008

The fifth Broadway production of *Gypsy,* this time starring
Patti LuPone, opens at the St. James Theater

June 15, 2008

SS is presented a Special Tony Award for
Lifetime Achievement in the Theater

September 30, 2008

The Story So Far..., a career-spanning box set celebrating the work
of Stephen Sondheim, is released in the US

November 18, 2008

An off-Broadway production of *Road Show,* a revision of the
show that tried out in Chicago and Washington as *Bounce,* opens
for a limited run at The Public Theater. It is directed by John
Doyle and stars Michael Cerveris and Alexander Gemignani

January 12, 2009

A Gala Concert reading of *A Little Night Music*
is presented at Studio 54 in New York

March 19, 2009

A Broadway revival of *West Side Story* opens at the
Palace Theater in New York

December 13, 2009

Based on the London production, a revival of *A Little Night
Music* opens on Broadway starring Catherine Zeta-Jones
as Desiree and Angela Lansbury as Madame Armfeldt. On
June 13, 2010, they are replaced by Bernadette Peters and
Elaine Stritch

March 15, 2010

Sondheim's 80th birthday is celebrated by the New York
Philharmonic at Lincoln Center. Several more celebrations are
held the following months: concerts by the Royal Philharmonic
in London in April, at the Kennedy Center in May, at the
Ravinia Festival near Chicago in July, and the BBC Proms at
London's Royal Albert Hall in July

March 22, 2010

On his birthday, SS learns that the former
Henry Miller's Theater on West 43rd Street has been
renamed the Stephen Sondheim Theater

April 8-11, 2010

Encores! presents a concert version of *Anyone Can Whistle*
starring Donna Murphy, Raul Esparza, and Sutton Foster

April 20, 2010
A DVD of *Evening Primrose* is commercially released

April 22, 2010
Sondheim on Sondheim, a multi-media revue of his work
conceived and directed by James Lapine, opens at the
Roundabout Theater for a limited run

October 26, 2010
The first part of Sondheim's collected lyrics, titled *Finishing
the Hat: Collected Lyrics (1954-1981) with Attendant Comments,
Principles, Heresies, Grudges, Whines, and Anecdotes,* is published
by Alfred A. Knopf

April 7-9, 2011
Staged concerts of *Company* directed by Lonny Price are
performed by the New York Philharmonic with Neil Patrick
Harris and Patti LuPone leading the cast

September 12, 2011
After a run at the Kennedy Center in Washington, a new
production of *Follies* opens on Broadway starring Bernadette
Peters, Jan Maxwell, Ron Raines, Danny Burstein, and
Elaine Paige

November 22, 2011
The second volume of SS's collected lyrics, *Look, I Made a
Hat: Collected Lyrics (1981-2011) with Attendant Comments,
Amplifications, Dogmas, Harangues, Digressions, Anecdotes, and
Miscellany,* is published

SONDHEIM & *Me*

February 8-19, 2012
Encores! at New York City Center presents a staged concert version of *Merrily We Roll Along* with Colin Donnell, Celia Keenan-Bolger, and Lin-Manuel Miranda

2013
Six by Sondheim, a documentary centering on the backstory of six Sondheim songs, airs on HBO. It is directed and co-produced by James Lapine

November 13–17, 2013
Sondheim collaborates with Wynton Marsalis on *A Bed and a Chair: A New York Love Affair,* an Encores! concert at New York City Center. It is directed by John Doyle and consists of more than two dozen Sondheim compositions

December 8, 2014
A film version of *Into the Woods* with Meryl Streep, James Gordon, and Emily Blunt has its world premiere in New York

November 24, 2015
Sondheim, Barbra Streisand, and Gloria Estefan are among the 17 American legends who accept the Presidential Medal of Freedom from President Barack Obama at the White House

May 11-15, 2016
Encores! presents a concert version of *Do I Hear a Waltz?* with Melissa Errico, Richard Troxell, Karen Ziemba, and Clayboune Elder

2017
SS marries Jeffrey Scott Romley

October 17, 2018

With Sondheim's approval, a revival of *Company* in the West End switches genders of several characters, and Bobby becomes Bobbie, played by Rosalie Craig. Directed by Marianne Elliott, the show also stars Patti LuPone as Joanne

July 24-27, 2019

Encores! Off-Center presents a concert version of *Road Show* starring Raul Esparza and Brandon Uranowitz

December 31, 2020

The New York Philharmonic presents a concert celebrating Sondheim's works. Hosted by Bernadette Peters, it is broadcast on PBS

April 26, 2020

Take Me to the World: A Sondheim 90th Birthday Celebration, a virtual concert featuring many celebrities singing his songs, is livestreamed

March 2, 2021

A Broadway transfer of the 2018 West End revival of *Company* opens for previews, but closes after nine performances because of the coronavirus pandemic. LuPone is the only holdover from the London cast, and Katrina Lenk now stars as Bobbie. Still directed by Marianne Elliott, the production resumes previews on November 15, 2021, and officially opens on December 9, 2021

September 15, 2021

SS tells Stephen Colbert on *The Late Show* that he is at work on a new show which he hopes to stage next season. It is being written with playwright David Ives and is entitled *Square One.* In an appearance on the *Today* show, Nathan Lane says he and Bernadette Peters participated in a reading of the show

November 2, 2021

After being delayed because of the pandemic, *Assassins,* directed by John Doyle, opens for previews Off-Broadway at the Classic Stage Company. Steven Pasquale, Will Swenson, and Judy Kuhn are in the cast

November 14-24, 2021

On November 14, 2021, SS attends the opening of the Off-Broadway revival of *Assassins.* On November 15, he attends a preview of the Broadway revival of *Company.* On November 24, he goes to a Wednesday matinee of *Is This a Room* and an evening performance of *Dana H,* two short plays on Broadway

November 26, 2021

Stephen Sondheim dies of cardiovascular disease at his home in Roxbury, Conn., after celebrating Thanksgiving with friends. He was 91

(Thanks to Michael H. Hutchins for his invaluable compilations.)

ACKNOWLEDGMENTS

This book could not have been written without the help of Amy Cooper Cary, head of Special Collections and University Archives in Raynor Memorial Libraries at Marquette University. Because I had donated all of my Sondheim material to the library, I had little at home, not even a complete set of *The Sondheim Review*. Amy cheerfully converted Sondheim's notes and faxes into PDFs and then lugged the magazines and boxes and boxes of photos to my home. Far beyond her normal duties and I am grateful.

Thanks must also be given to those who put out *The Sondheim Review* year after year. First, our designer, the tireless Molly Quirk, who tolerated my vague directions and last-minute changes to produce a very classy magazine.

All of the editors and writers are too numerous to mention individually, but special thanks to editors Marley Brenman Korn, Eric Grode, David Wirthwein, and Rick Pender; to writers Sean Patrick Flahaven, who reported on Sondheim in New York, and Terri Roberts, who covered Los Angeles news like the proverbial blanket, and to John Olson, Scott Ross, Suzanne Bixby, Joanne Gordon, Mark Eden Horowitz, Wayman Wong, Susan Weir, Bonnie Weiss, Frank Rizzo, Ken Mandelbaum, Mark Shenton, Graham Coppin, and Michael Buckley. I'm "always grateful."

I also want to thank two Loyola University Maryland interns—Jackie Alvarez-Hernandez and Jason Arthur. They were loaned to me by my publisher, Bancroft Press, and their help on, and enthusiasm for, this book project was invaluable. I always must thank Tracy Copes, who designed both the book cover and the book interior—inspired efforts both, in my opinion.

And an extra special thanks to Barbara Salsini, who not only edited stories but also kept the editor calm during hectic days.

ABOUT THE *Author*

Aprolific and versatile writer, Paul Salsini was a reporter and editor at *The Milwaukee Journal* for thirty-seven years and the Wisconsin correspondent for *The New York Times* for fifteen years. He taught journalism courses at his alma mater, Marquette University, for many years.

As someone knowledgeable about musical theater, he also taught the History of Musical Theater course at Marquette. In 1994, he founded *The Sondheim Review*, a magazine devoted to the works of the composer/lyricist, and was its editor for ten years.

In recent years, he has written fiction set in Tuscany, including the six-volume, award-winning "A Tuscan Series." His latest book, *A Tuscan Treasury: Stories from Italy's Most Captivating Region*, was published in 2021.

He and his wife, Barbara, have three children, Jim, Laura and Jack, and four grandchildren and live in Milwaukee with their cat, Rosie.

BOOK CLUB
QUESTIONS

1. Before reading *Sondheim & Me*, how well did you know Stephen Sondheim and his work?

2. What are some of your favorite plays/musicals?

3. Did the memoir change your opinion of Sondheim and his work? How?

4. Was there anything in Salsini's memoir that surprised you?

5. Sondheim went out of his way to send Salsini items such as sheet music and videotapes. What do you think this says about his character?

6. Sondheim was surprised at the idea of a magazine being dedicated to him and his work. Why do you think he decided to let Salsini start the magazine?

7. The memoir features not only excerpts from Sondheim himself, but also individuals who worked with him, such as James Lapine and Marin Mazzie. Do you think they added to the memoir, or should it have been focused solely on Sondheim's words?

8. In the chapter titled "Some 'Juvenilia," Sondheim goes out of his way to tell Salsini he would have preferred his high school work to have not been published in the magazine. Discuss whether Salsini should have kept the juvenilia out of the magazine or if he was right to include it.

9. How did you feel about Sondheim giving Salsini his phone numbers and claiming they "might as well be on a first-name basis"? Do you think Salsini earned his trust, or was there a different reason?

10. After the first issue is published, Sondheim sends Salsini some "corrections and elucidations." What did you think of this practice of Sondheim's?

11. Sondheim at one point gives his opinion on the film versions of his musicals. What's your opinion of film musicals—do they work, or not? Why?

12. Salsini receives a very intense phone call from Sondheim after the magazine's review of *Passion* is published. Was Sondheim justified in his anger? How would you have reacted if you had been Salsini?

13. To this day, Salsini still has no idea why Sondheim reacted the way he did to the review. Discuss some possible explanations for Sondheim's reaction.

14. What did you think of Sondheim's answers to the interviews? Was there anything that stood out to you?

15. Salsini decides to include a chapter about the translated versions of Sondheim's shows in other countries. Why do you think he did so? How do you feel about the translations?

16. After Salsini retires from his position as editor and publisher, he and Sondheim don't have as much contact. Do you think Salsini should've tried to keep in touch, or was it best to remain distant?

17. Do you think Salsini portrayed Sondheim accurately? Why or why not?

18. Would Sondheim agree with you? Why or why not?

19. What do you think Sondheim would say if he could read Salsini's memoir?

20. Salsini writes that he "didn't want this to be simply Sondheim AND *The Sondheim Review*. [He] wanted it to be Sondheim IN *The Sondheim Review*". Do you think he succeeded in doing so?

Compiled by Jackie Alvarez-Hernandez

Index

Christin, Judith, 145

Church, Forrest, 109, 110

Clark, Victoria, 202

Colbert, Stephen, 207

Collins, Dorothy, 67, 149, 190

Collins, Judy, 191

Company, 5, 38, 39, 41, 45, 49-52, 58-59, 61, 91, 97, 109, 117, 129-130 134, 136, 146, 157, 160, 162-164, 177, 182, 189,190, 195, 197, 202, 205, 207, 208

Corrigan, Peter, 88

Creel, Gavin, 168

Crosby, Kim, 194

Crossword puzzles, 62, 189

Cuervo, Alma,175

Daly, Tyne, 153, 194

Danner, Blythe, 117-121, 199

Dartmouth College, 141

De Carlo, Yvonne, 67-69, 149, 190

Dench, Judi, 104

Depp, Johnny, 203

Dick Tracy, 194-195

Do I Hear a Waltz?, 3-4, 39, 46-47, 107, 182, 188, 206

Donnell, Colin, 206

Doyle, John, 175, 202-203, 206

Elder, Claybourne, 175, 206

Elliott, Patricia, 103-104

Ellis, Scott, 49-50, 183

Epstein, Julius, 83

Epstein, Philip, 81, 83

Errico, Melissa, 129-130, 206

Esparza, Raul, 129-130, 202, 204, 207

Estefan, Gloria, 206

Evans, Daniel, 199, 203

Evans, Harvey, 108, 149-152

Evening Primrose, 22, 94, 107, 189

(The) Exception and the Rule, 189

Flahaven, Sean Patrick, 93, 125, 133

Follies, 4-5, 38, 48, 67-69, 71-76, 97, 101, 117-122, 126, 149-152, 177, 188, 190, 193, 194, 199, 202, 205

Ford, Paul, 81, 183

Foster, Sutton, 204

Fowler, Beth, 194

Fox, Janet, 185

Franchi, Sergio, 188

Francolini, Anna, 86

Friedman, Maria, 57, 194

(The) Frogs, 39, 178, 182, 191, 200, 201

Furth, George, 45, 51, 53, 189, 192, 197

Gaines, Boyd, 49, 50, 197

Garber, Victor, 195, 198, 202

Garrett, Betty, 122

Gelbart, Larry, 54-56, 188

Gemignani, Alexander, 175, 203

Gemignani, Paul, 96, 145, 183

George School, 61, 77, 185

Getting Away with Murder, 45, 53, 177-178, 197

Gingold, Hermione, 190